PRAISE FOR

GodChicks and the Men They Love

This is one of the finest relationship books that I have read in a long time. Holly and Philip Wagner are a delightfully authentic couple who made me laugh, think, rethink and put into practice their excellent ideas. Their writing and communication style is fresh, spontaneous and extremely practical. I highly recommend this book.

Dr. Jim Burns, Ph.D.
President of HomeWord, Author of *Creating an Intimate Marriage* and
Closer: Devotions to Draw Couples Closer Together

I am so excited that you have this book in your hands. Philip and Holly are not only one of the best teaching couples on relationships, but they also work hard to live out the principles outlined in this book. You will find practical tools to help you go higher in every level of your relationships, and you will laugh as you learn from their own journey. I highly welcome and recommend this great book.

Christine and Nick Caine
Author, Speakers and Founders of A21

Real, raw and straight shootin'! Holly and Philip do not hold back! What a great book to teach from. I plan on using this at our church and, if I can remember to do so, I'll give proper credit to the authors . . . lol!

Ted Cunningham
Co-author of *From Anger to Intimacy*, *As Long as We Both Shall Live* and
The Language of Sex

Philip and Holly Wagner have a teaching style unlike any other—they live and teach out of a dynamic relationship with both God and each other. Philip and Holly are dear friends of ours, and their perspective on healthy relationships and maintaining a fun, God-centered marriage is refreshing. Their humorous writing style and passion for people will captivate your mind and challenge your heart as we all seek for God's leading in this important area of life.

Brian and Bobbie Houston
Senior Pastors of Hillsong Church, Australia

We all want it—the fairytale ending, "they lived happily ever after"—yet most of us don't know how to get it. Philip and Holly Wagner know how to help. Their honest and humorous approach to the desire of all of our hearts is a practical and personal how-to that we all desperately need.

Debbie and Robert Morris
Senior Pastor of Gateway Church, Austin, Texas
Bestselling Author of *The Blessed Life*

Relationships can be a tangled web of heartache if not navigated with precaution and care. From the nerve-wracking first date to the covenanted walk down the aisle, men and women have to take time to lean in, listen carefully, learn and make wise decisions. Pastors Philip and Holly have given the body of Christ a gift—not just with this book but also with their lives. Their own marriage has mentored and encouraged many others—including my own. What they have penned in these pages is a must-read for everyone who wants to reap a maximum harvest in his or her relationship.

Priscilla Shirer
Bible Teacher and Author

I have been teaching the differences of men and women since the 1970s. This book is so refreshing in how it honors those differences. Thank you, Holly and Philip, for being real and sharing your life on every page.

Gary Smalley
Bestselling Co-author of *From Anger to Intimacy, As Long as We Both Shall Live* and *The Language of Sex*

When we dream of the perfect relationship, we often imagine the trust, excitement and security of a lifelong commitment. In reality, we know that a truly successful relationship takes work, dedication and a willingness to humble ourselves and learn. In this book, our good friends Philip and Holly Wagner spotlight the journey that successful relationships must experience—a journey that they have been travelling themselves for more than 25 years. Whether you are single, dating or have been married for decades, throughout these pages you will encounter more than relational advice or quick fixes. Instead, you will discover the scriptural truths that will help reawaken you to God's desire for your life and your relationship.

Ed and Lisa Young
Pastor of Fellowship Church, Grapevine, Texas
Authors of *The Creative Marriage* and *The Marriage Mirror*

GodChicks and the Men They Love

Holly + Philip **Wagner**

GodChicks

and the Men They Love

Regal

From Gospel Light
Ventura, California, U.S.A.

Published by Regal
From Gospel Light
Ventura, California, U.S.A.
www.regalbooks.com
Printed in the U.S.A.

Library of Congress Cataloging-in-Publication Data
Wagner, Holly.
Godchicks and the men they love / Holly Wagner, Philip Wagner.
p. cm.
Includes bibliographical references.
ISBN 978-0-8307-5238-6 (trade paper)
1. Wives—Religious life. 2. Marriage—Religious aspects—Christianity.
3. Man-woman relationships—Religious aspects—Christianity. I. Wagner, Philip, 1953-
II. Title. III. Title: God chicks and the men they love.
BV4528.15.W34 2010
248.8'44—dc22
2009049117

Rights for publishing this book outside the U.S.A. or in non-English languages are
administered by Gospel Light Worldwide, an international not-for-profit ministry.
For additional information, please visit www.glww.org, email info@glww.org, or write to
Gospel Light Worldwide, 1957 Eastman Avenue, Ventura, CA 93003, U.S.A.

Dedicated . . .
To all of you committed to doing the work
required to have amazing relationships

Contents

Thanks to . . .

So many people who have helped us navigate our own marriage (some of whom we may never meet), including:

Gary Smalley—for helping us understand that our differences can make our marriage stronger . . .

Gary Chapman—for helping us speak each other's language . . .

Neil Clark Warren—for insights on people and on qualities to look for in a great mate . . .

Ashley—for reading through the initial manuscript so quickly and correcting the typos and other glitches . . .

Our Oasis family—for wanting to learn about relationships, and for being patient with us as we have taught about building them over the years . . .

Jordan and Paris, our children—for keeping life exciting and love-filled . . .

Most of the time, we thank God for each other . . . and always, we thank Him for the privilege of being shepherds in His house.

Introduction

Thoughts from Holly

I don't think I actually "fell in love" with Philip.

It was more like growing in love.

I just remember my heart beating harder when I was with him.

I remember wanting to spend every moment with him.

I remember loving him as I played his newly recorded album (on LP and cassette, not CD . . . we are old).

I remember being inspired by his relationship with God. It just seemed so easy and so real.

I loved (and still do) listening to him teach. He made (and still makes) the Bible seem practical and relevant.

I loved how compassionate, patient and non-judgmental he was (and still is) with people.

I loved how he made (and still makes) me laugh. No one makes me laugh like him.

I know him far better now than I did when we first began our journey. And I love him more. We have learned how to value and honor each other. We have gotten better and better at communicating in a way that builds. We have learned how to appreciate where we are different. We have learned patience. We have realized that together we are stronger.

That said, there have been moments along our journey when he drove me nuts, when I questioned my choice of husband.

"Remind me that divorce is expensive and that murder is against the law," was a plea I made to a friend a number of years ago. I laugh about that comment now, but back then I wasn't kidding! At that time, our marriage wasn't fun, maintaining it was so much work and he didn't "understand me!"

Perhaps there have been times when you have felt like that. You vaguely remember those lovin' feelings . . . you're just not having them now.

Well, take heart. You are not alone.

Or maybe you are single and you don't really want to be.

Maybe your friends are getting married and your closet is full of bridesmaid's dresses. Perhaps the movie *27 Dresses* is not fiction but reality for you, and you are debating whether or not you should just settle. You are wondering if there is a man out there for you.

Well, yes . . . there is.

You might just have to do some work.

On you.

And on what you are looking for. Yeah, there are still great men out there. And there are some men you shouldn't touch with a 10-foot pole. Hopefully this book can help you tell the difference.

After 25 years of building a marriage, of navigating some of the tricky curves, Philip and I want to share a little of what we have learned.

One of the last prayers Jesus prayed was that we, all of humanity, would become one. Sounds a lot easier than it is! If we, humanity, are going to become one, it will probably start in our homes.

One of the definitions of the word "extreme" is "farthest removed from ordinary or average."

I like that.

You and I need to be *extreme* people in just about every area of our lives. And certainly in our relationships! *Average* marriages are failing at an alarming rate. So how about if we become *extreme* in our commitment to build a marriage? How about if we become *extreme* in our determination to understand more than be understood?

So much of our lives are spent navigating the ever-tricky road of relationships. And some of us (not you, of course!) have made very stupid decisions when it comes to the men we let into our hearts. While we may never become experts on the whole relationship thing, I do think we could all get a little better at it.

That is the heart of this book.

Our hope and prayer is that it helps you.

Philip and I will alternate chapters. On some subjects, you will hear from both of us, just with a different perspective. His chapters will definitely be more organized.

This shouldn't be a surprise!

Introduction

Thoughts from Philip

Women are a gift to the human race.

But humanity has a way of mistreating the gifts given to us. Women are a secret weapon and the keys to fully enjoying life. They have become God's secret weapon: GodChicks. Women who love God recognize their own worth as a treasure and sense a calling to make a difference in the world.

GodChicks are a secret weapon to bring hope, comfort and life to most any situation. It's not that big of a secret, really. Some people just aren't paying attention.

There are no manuals on loving women well (a lot of people don't like to read manuals anyway). And while we may not, historically, have always been kind to women, I believe it's time for us to change the game plan. It's time to right a wrong.

It's time for us to honor the girls!

Women flourish when they are honored and empowered by the men in their world. Men often don't realize the impact they have on a woman's soul. Dads underestimate their mark on their daughters. Brothers underestimate their influence on their sisters. Boyfriends are often oblivious to the marks that will remain on the souls of the girls they date. And husbands don't realize the importance of their touch in the heart of their wives.

I've heard it said that a woman's skin is 10 times more sensitive to touch than a man's.

Ten times more sensitive to a cold touch, a selfish touch, a warm and encouraging touch, a harmful touch, a non-sexual touch and a sensual touch. (Keep in mind that touch can be physical, emotional or verbal.)

Listen to the powerful impact of a tender touch:

> 'Twas not into my ear you whispered
> But into my heart
> 'Twas not my lips you kissed
> But my soul.

JUDY GARLAND, "MY LOVE IS LOST"[1]

You should be kissed and often . . . and by someone who knows how.
RHETT BUTLER, *GONE WITH THE WIND*

Notice the tone of the man's version of a kiss and the tone of the woman's version. It can seem like everything about us is different.

In this book, we will look at how men and women, despite our varying idiosyncrasies, can work together to make a difference in our world and can build an alliance that brings fulfillment to us all.

Reading this book will hopefully help you understand the man you love a bit better. Men are different than women. Men are not your enemy; they are just different. And the key to a better relationship is understanding.

I don't represent all men. I'm not the spokesman for the whole team here. I'm just one man, one voice trying to explain, trying to bridge the gap between women and the men they love—and who love them back. Hopefully you will understand more, maybe laugh a bit and enjoy relationships a little more, after you read this book.

The better we understand each other, the less likely we are to look at each other and think, *What is wrong with you?*

The Relationship Dance

A great relationship is like a dance. You have a partner. You want to enjoy the experience, enjoy the journey and step on each other's toes as little as possible.

Dancing is part technique and part chemistry. It is both learning the basic moves and letting the music take you.

It took awhile for me to figure out that my wife, Holly, was a gift to me.

At first I was smitten. We were so in love. But soon I had my doubts that she was actually a gift—I mean, we were and are so different . . .

When she's hot, I'm cold; when I'm too warm, she's too cold. She wants to go faster; I want to slow things down for a minute. She doesn't just walk to the beat of a different drummer; sometimes it's a different song altogether.

She and I see most things differently.

We used to try to change each other. We got so frustrated.

But we finally got it. We are a team. Twenty-five years later, we recognize that her strengths make us better and stronger. My strengths make us wiser. A major change in our relationship occurred when we started to recognize the differences, accept our differences and find a way to respect the differences. You will read a lot about that in this book.

Take the "Five-Minute Issue," for instance. When we are getting ready to go out, it takes me 10 minutes—12 minutes tops, if I'm also doing my hair. Holly needs a lot more time, which is not the issue.

Here is where the problem starts: I'm more literal, while she is more metaphorical. I like to be on time, which to me means 5 to 10 minutes early. Holly takes "on time" with a more metaphorical interpretation.

"Holly, are you ready to go?"

"I'm ready," she says.

I think she means that she's ready now, so I go down and start the car. But she doesn't really mean that she is ready to go now—like *right now*. Her *now* is in more like, say, 5 minutes. So why doesn't she just say "in about 5 minutes"? Even if she did, she wouldn't mean 5 *actual* minutes. It's more general than that.

I get frustrated.

Then she reminds me, "Five minutes. You know, like the 5 minutes you tell me are left in the basketball game. Which is more like 15 or 20."

"Oh. Right. Good point."

Driving in silence is a common experience when you are trying to figure *Who am I married to?* and *What just happened?* The key is understanding . . . and patience.

Keeping your eye on the big picture, on the vision for your life, is important. That will help you navigate through many little battles. Otherwise, it's easy to get stuck on little issues that can sour the relationship. You are not going to understand everything about men. They are not going to understand everything about you.

Like "The Chewing Issue." We are sitting in bed reading at the end of the night. My wife is snacking. She is eating some kind of chips. It is the loudest noise I've heard all day.

"Excuse me, do you think you can chew more quietly?"

"I'm just chewing. There's no volume on chewing," she defends.

"How can that much noise—" I suddenly realize I'm heading into dangerous waters "—come out of such a cute . . . jaw? I'm not criticizing, I'm just saying . . ."

"Just read. Stop picking on me."

"Sorry."

She reads few more minutes, closes her book and turns out her lamp.

"Are you going to read much longer?" she asks. "Because the light bothers me."

"I'm reading Grisham; just a couple more chapters. Does the light bother you?"

"Of course it bothers me . . ." and then she says a couple of sentences that are too low for me to hear.

"What?"

She repeats what she said, only at a lower volume.

"Are you mumbling or did you have something you wanted to say?"

"Goodnight, Philip."

"So . . . there will be no sex tonight, then?" I try to stop the words before they come out of my mouth but—too late.

We both stare up at the ceiling, thinking, *God, help me understand this person lying next to me.*

We can let these little annoying interactions define who we are and our relationship, or we can have a greater purpose and vision in mind—like unity and fulfilling God's purpose.

Someone told me that men don't often read relationship books. I'm writing my portion of this book primarily to women, but I hope that the man in your life will at least read the "Just for the Men!" section at the end of every chapter. I believe it will help him gain understanding that will bring strength to both your lives—you, a GodChick, and the man you love.

And off we go . . .

Note

1. Judy Garland, "My Love Is Lost," from an unpublished collection of poems, 1939.

1

Mirror, Mirror on the Wall

(Holly)

It is your moral obligation to be happy.[1]
DR. LAURA SCHLESSINGER

I praise You for I am fearfully and wonderfully made.
PSALM 139

It is not your husband's job to give you a life. It is not his job to make you feel good about yourself.

Jesus told us that we are to love our neighbors as we love ourselves (see Luke 10:27). Maybe we do . . . and that's the problem.

We may not really love who we are, so we may not be that great at loving anyone else. And loving people is why we are here. You and I are supposed to be the human expression of God's love to this very hurting world. We will never be able to do that if we don't love ourselves.

There are some big reasons why we must love ourselves.

One of the biggest is that it's very hard for others to love the real us when we're trying to be someone else.

We all need to grow and make changes. When dating, however, we need to be careful that we don't try to change who we really are. I have overheard dating couples having conversations that go something like this:

"Do you like to travel?"
"Oh yes, I really like to travel." (I know she hates it.)
"Do you like Thai food?"
"Yes, I love it." (Again, I know that she doesn't like it.)
"I really love classical music."

"Me too." (No, she doesn't. She is lying. She is seriously into country.)

They are setting the other person up.

Why? Because they are not comfortable with who they are and are trying, instead, to be who the other person might want. That gets confusing.

Julia Roberts's character in *Runaway Bride* has this very problem. She doesn't really like herself, so she tries to be whoever the man she is dating wants her to be. She doesn't even know how she likes her eggs; she eats them cooked however the man she is with prefers them. Not good. It's only after she takes a little time to figure herself out that she is ready to commit to a marriage.

Just be yourself.

There are plenty of people who will think you are wonderful.

Be who you are.

Don't waste your time, or the other person's, by setting him up.

Another reason why we must love ourselves is that, if we don't, we will choose bad men to marry. We are more likely to settle for less, even accepting mistreatment, because we feel we don't deserve better.

You are a daughter of the King! You have the right to aim high when choosing a date or a spouse . . . but you won't if you don't love yourself.

That said, let's keep a level head. Brace yourself. There is no perfect guy or girl out there. Movies and fairy tales spoil us, but we have to learn to navigate the reality of our human nature in light of God's best for us. We are all on a journey, so if you are waiting for Mr. Perfect, forget it.

But you don't have to accept Mr. Way-Below-Average either.

Nope.

Let him grow up first.

I like being around people who are confident.

Not arrogant.

Arrogance is unattractive and ugly, and often is a mask for insecurity.

But quiet confidence is great.

Someone who can laugh at himself and can take a joke, without getting his feelings hurt, is worth waiting for.

Do the Math

When you like who you are, you're not overly needy.

It is hard to build intimacy with someone who is needy. Needy people are exhausting. And they make very bad choices in relationships. There was a pop song by Mariah Carey on the radio every five minutes not too long ago. The lyrics moan, "I can't live if living is without you!"[2]

It sounds so tragically romantic to say that losing your lover or their affection would make life unlivable.

But it is not healthy.

I can live without Philip. I don't want to, because I love doing life with him. And we are planning on growing old together. But because I know who I am, and like who I am, the truth is . . . I could live without him. This makes me not a needy person. I don't look to him to give me a purpose to live.

God calls us to be interdependent on each other. By definition, that means "mutually dependent." We should engage in reciprocal relationship with our mate and reserve our dependence for God alone. Only God can be our everything, because He alone is perfect. He gives us purpose, destiny and a reason to live. My husband is not perfect (pretty close!), so I look to God for my purpose to live, not to Philip. That's too much pressure for our spouse to handle. He is not designed to carry that load.

We are created for partnership.

In the movie *Jerry Maguire*, Tom Cruise's character says to the love of his life, "You complete me." Now, that certainly sounds romantic, and we probably all sighed when we heard it. But honestly, that is nonsense.

We shouldn't be looking for someone to complete us.

You are not some fragmented woman looking for a man to fill the gaps. God didn't create you as a half. A healthy relationship is when two wholes come together. The goal is for you and me to be wholes.

When God told Adam that it wasn't good for him to be alone (see Gen. 2:18), He created the woman, Eve, as a partner. She was not created to be a drain.

Solomon said that two are better than one (see Eccles. 4:9).

Doing the math, that means that $1 + 1 = 2$.

By way of contrast, ½ + ½ = 1 . . . which is less than 2. One is the same number God started with, which means this "partnership" of two halves will not further the purpose of heaven on the earth the way two whole persons coming together can. The purpose of marriage is to glorify God, to be the example of love between Him and His Church (see Eph. 5:32). Two whole people can engage in a mutually dependent relationship with honest, open and vulnerable communication and accountability, while encouraging and urging each other further and deeper into the purpose of God. Like Eve, you are designed to bring help and companionship to your relationship.

Two halves united together typically experience false intimacy, veins of co-dependency, secrets, hiding, miscommunication and fear about each other's purpose and destiny. It is very hard to encourage your mate to become who they are in God when you aren't sure who you are in Him.

My ability to like myself does not come from thinking I am so wonderful, but from God thinking it (see Ps. 139:14). I am His masterpiece, His one-of-a-kind creation (see Eph. 2:10). And honestly, the deepest needs of my soul are met by my God. I have an honest and real relationship with my Creator. I do not expect Philip to meet needs that only God can.

Now, I am not saying you don't have needs that your spouse is supposed to meet. Men actually like to meet a woman's needs. Philip often helps me fix things. (I don't mean he fixes things around the house, because he doesn't. If it takes more than a hammer or WD-40, we have to call someone.) He helps me when I need to clarify a teaching message, or to negotiate the emotions involved in girlfriend-ship, or to organize my sometimes-scattered thoughts. There were a few times as I navigated my breast cancer battle that he helped me conquer fear, reminding me what God says about healing. When I needed reassurance, he gave it. When I needed someone to hold me in the doctor's office, he did.

And he needs me. To find things. To encourage him. To introduce him to new people. To play. Together, Philip and I have accomplished far more than either of us could have alone.

I am not saying that we don't have legitimate needs. We all do, and our spouse can meet them. But having needs and being needy are two different things. And that is the point I am trying to make.

Neediness demands. Having needs asks.

Independent . . . not good.

Dependent . . . not good.

Interdependent . . . *good*.

When we don't like who we are, then we are constantly looking for someone else to fill us up. And while Philip can certainly be an encourager—as he should be—he is not responsible for how I see myself.

There might be a lot of reasons for our insecurity—past abuse, neglect, rejection or abandonment. All of us, to one degree or another, have experienced at least one of these. Nevertheless, at some point, we must begin to believe that we are who God says we are . . . and to live our lives out of that knowledge.

I heard someone say once, "If I get hit by a truck, it's not my fault; but it is my responsibility to learn to walk again." We have to face our past, our issues, our hurts and wounds, if we desire to be a great mate. We have to take responsibility—not the blame, but the responsibility to heal, grow and change into a healthy individual rooted in God's love and in His Word.

Who Are You?

There are about five billion of us on the planet who believe in God. That's good. But we need to take that belief one step further, and not only believe in God, but also believe that He created us for a purpose.

You are not an accident.

No matter what your parents told you, you were put on the planet at this time in history for a specific reason. God plucked you out of eternity and entrusted you with this time in history.

He could have had you born at any time, but He chose now.

There must be a reason. You have a purpose and a destiny to live out. And we really won't know our purpose if we don't know our Creator.

If I want to know specifics about my Prius, I don't ask another car. I ask the company that made the car. I have had to read the manual a few times as I have learned all about my new hybrid.

The first step toward liking yourself is knowing that you were created for a purpose, and that it is a good one.

Knowing that you are the loved-beyond-measure daughter of the King changes everything. We're women! We know love changes everything!

You can learn God's ways and mature into loving His character as you realize that He is not the sum of your human experience. In other words, He is not who your earthly father was, who your abuser was, who your backbiting, critical ex-boyfriends were. That is not His character. His character is good.

The next step is to discover who He is, who you are in Him and what your purpose is. You can do this by getting to know your Creator, by reading His manual. The Word of God, the Bible, is His love letter to you, His instruction manual for you. It's not a rulebook with impossible standards that you can never live up to; it's an expression of love that communicates and propels you forward into His very best.

Another reason we must know who we are is to determine what we'll do. We can't do this backward. I can't rely on what I do to determine who I am, because if what I do is snatched away or if I fail at it, then I'll see myself as a loser. LeBron James is an amazing basketball player, but what happens when he can no longer play? What about the Julia Robertses and Luciano Pavarottis of the world? What happens when they can no longer do what they do? Will they be confused or depressed? Will they take it out on their loved ones?

What about you?

Is your identity wrapped up in what you do?

Before you were a wife, mother, teacher or lawyer, you were a loved-beyond-measure, perfectly created daughter of the King.

We don't get our identity from our driver's license. Most of the stuff on there is wrong. I certainly don't weigh what it says I weigh! And I actually think my address has changed!

We don't get our identity from our passport (that just tells us where we have been).

We don't get our identity from school report cards (many of us might still be dealing with some negative stuff teachers said!).

We don't get our identity from a mirror (that's just what we use to put makeup on).

You and I get our identity from our Creator.

It is through His eyes that we get a true picture of the individuals we are.

Here is some of what our amazing God has to say about us.

All you have to do is believe it.

Maybe saying it out loud will help.

I am a child of God (see John 1:2).
I am a joint-heir with Christ (see Rom. 8:17).
I am the daughter of the King (see Ps. 45).
I am called (see Jer. 1:5).
I am purposed (see Eph. 2:10).
I am chosen (see Eph. 1:11).
I am fearfully and wonderfully made (see Ps. 139:13-14).
I am equipped for battle (see Eph. 6:10-17).
I am more than a conqueror (see Rom. 8:17).
I am a part of God's plan for justice on the earth (see Isa. 61:1).
I am the righteousness of God in Christ (see 2 Cor. 5:21).
I am free from condemnation (see Rom. 8:1).
I am the temple of the Holy Spirit (see 1 Cor. 6:19).
I am free from sickness and disease (see Matt. 8:17).
I am delivered from sin (see Rom. 6:7; John 3:16).
I am accepted in Him (see Eph. 1:5-7).
I am loved beyond measure (see John 17:23).
I am complete in Him (see Col. 2:10).
I am a new creation in Christ Jesus (see 2 Cor. 5:17).
I am adopted by God and translated into His kingdom (see
   Rom. 8:15; Col. 1:13).
I am training the next generation to live well (see Titus 2:3-5).
I am delivered from the power of darkness (see Col. 1:13).
I am an ambassador for Christ (see 2 Cor. 5:20).
I am saved by grace (see Eph. 2:8-9).
I am created to bring glory to God (see 2 Cor. 3:17-18;
   Col. 1:15-17).
I am living to honor and worship God (see Rom. 12:1).
I am transformed by the renewing of my mind
   (see Rom. 12:2).
I am redeemed from the curse of the law (see Gal. 3:13).
I am in Christ (see 1 Cor. 1:30; Col. 3:3).
I am the will of God (see Jas. 1:18; Rev. 4:11).

I am completely loved, completely accepted, completely forgiven
and complete in Him. I am the will of God.
    Seeing ourselves as He sees us is a primary step on the journey of
loving ourselves.

Set a Goal and Go for It!

There are some other steps we can take.

Setting a goal and overcoming all the obstacles on the way to reaching it will do great things for how we see ourselves. Not only does it feel great to meet a goal we have set, but it's also a great way to build endurance . . . and to learn a little word called *tenacity*. It takes a proactive, do-whatever-it-takes attitude to meet a goal.

During my 25 years as a pastor, I have talked with so many young women who have struggled with this issue of identity.

Change for them has begun with starting to see themselves through God's eyes.

Change has continued with setting a goal and reaching it.

I talk to many young women with various addictions—sex, drugs, food, shopping.

They see themselves as failures.

And as long as they do, they will never be free.

But once they see themselves as loved by God and reach just one goal, they are well on the way to health.

For some, the goal was getting a "sobriety job"—regular hours, showing up when they were supposed to, and being accountable to someone.

For others, it was finishing school.

For some, it was taking an exercise class and showing up every week.

For others, it was losing 50 pounds.

A weakness of mine was that I didn't always finish the projects I started. I am a great starter . . . it is just my finishing that needs work! Being weak in this area affected how I saw myself. I knew that I needed to start something and finish it. And it needed to be something significant. Something other than finishing a book or a triple-scoop cone!

At that time in my life I was taking my son, Jordan, to karate class. As I watched the classes, I began to think, *I can do this.* Plus, I noticed that at every level a student passed, a new color of belt was given, all the way to the black belt.

It was like a prize, and I like prizes.

So I signed up for karate.

Perhaps that wasn't the easiest of goals for me to reach, but that was what I did. The first day of class, I showed up in my new white uniform and stiff white belt. I was so excited because I had seen the movie *Karate Kid* and I wanted to learn to do the amazing kick from the end of the movie. I just knew it wouldn't be long before I wowed my family and friends with my incredible ability.

Well, we didn't learn that amazing kick the first day. Or even the fortieth day.

Bummer!

For months, we learned how to fall.

This was not what I signed up for!

I spent hours learning how to fall to the front, how to fall on my back, how to fall to the side.

Fall. Get up. Fall. Get up. Fall. Get up.

Boring!

To be completely honest, I wanted to quit.

But that had been my pattern for years.

As soon as a project got a little mundane or slightly boring, I would quit, feeling justified . . . because why should I have to put up with boring? And then I would look for something more exciting.

Here's a tip for free: Sometimes life, marriage and work are boring. They become routine. Because we are grown-ups, the decisions we make during those times actually say a lot about our character. Previously, the decisions I made during the boring part of projects revealed that I was a quitter.

But this time I didn't quit.

I kept the goal of a black belt in front of me.

A few years into the karate challenge, my son decided that he wanted to devote most of his time to basketball. He no longer wanted to study karate.

Great.

Now my karate goal became an inconvenience.

It wasn't easy to figure out what to do with the rest of the family while I continued to take classes. I almost quit at that point.

Another tip for free: Reaching goals is never convenient.

Three years into my study of karate, it began to get physically difficult. The moves I was required to learn were tough. The forms (a series of intricate movements) I had to memorize were so complicated, that I wondered if my goal of getting a black belt was too hard a goal for me. Karate is a contact sport, and that was becoming more and more evident—we were sparring by this point in my training, and I ended up with more bruises than I wanted.

Last tip for free: Any worthwhile goal is difficult and can be painful to reach.

Four and a half years later, I passed my black-belt test.

Yippee!!!

Were there times when it had been boring?

Yes.

Were there times it was inconvenient?

Yes.

Were there times when it seemed too difficult?

Yes.

Just the fact that it *was* a difficult goal to finish made it even more valuable to me. Getting my black belt did things for how I saw myself that nothing else had done up to that point.

I had started something.

And finished it.

You can, too. Pick something, anything. Find a goal and begin the process of reaching it, overcoming the obstacles on the way: boredom, inconvenience, difficulty, and others. When you finally get there, even with all the bumps and bruises, you will feel amazing! Your confidence will soar as you allow life to extract the potential lying dormant or unknown from inside you. You will realize that there is so much more on the inside of you than you originally thought.

Are you enjoying your life?

I'm sure there are challenging moments, but are you basically happy? Are you interesting? Or do you bore even yourself?

It is so much easier to be around someone interesting—someone who is passionate about something . . . *anything.* Do you have a hobby you are invested in or a cause you are fighting for?

If your biggest interest is in finding or keeping a man, you are not very interesting. And no man will think so either.

When we like who we are, we engage with the world. We read books. We have interests. We have hobbies. We love life!

Green (with Envy) Isn't Your Color

When a woman is confident in her purpose and has a healthy image of herself, she has no occasion or time for envy. Think about it. Why do we get jealous of others? Usually because we want what they have without paying the cost they paid to have it, and because we aren't truly enjoying who we are.

I can't sing.

Not one note in key.

I have tried. I have taken lessons. Which is why I am always amazed at those who can really sing.

I also can't draw.

Not at all.

Stick figures are the extent of my portrait ability. Art classes did not help. I am in awe of those artists on the street who can draw a portrait in about 10 minutes.

Given these realities, I have a choice. I can be envious of those people who can sing and draw, or I can be happy there are people on the planet to whom God has entrusted those gifts and be thankful for the gifts He's given me.

None of us were created with the exact same purposes, personalities or destinies. Each of us is unique. Each of us needs to spend time discovering who she is and what her purpose is, instead of trying to be like someone else and wanting her gifts. That will only lead to frustration and envy.

Someone who truly likes herself can rejoice when a friend lands a job, gets married or is offered an amazing opportunity.

God's opportunities are limitless—He has great things in store for you, too. Just keep walking on the path He has assigned to you, and keep discovering *why* you are here. The doors God plans for you to walk through will not require that you break them down. He will open them for you. You just have to be ready, not distracted by someone else's open door. Get great at celebrating the successes of others at home, at work and in your friendship circle. Life is so much better when our security rests in Him.

Proverbs 31 celebrates the "virtuous woman." That is a great word. Its root means "a force on the earth." You and I are designed to be a force on the earth.

A force on the earth for good.

We are designed to make a difference.

To be a part of the solution.

And we are designed to be this force before a man even enters the picture. The challenge for the man, according to that chapter of Proverbs, is to find us. To find the virtuous woman.

I am not to wait for a man, including my husband, to make me virtuous. That responsibility is in my lap. Remember: Marriage is a place for two wholes to meet, not a place to get neediness met.

Happiness Is Simple

Part of being comfortable in our own skin is making the decision to be uncomplicated. I got a letter a few years ago from my friend Bobbie. In it she wrote, "Holly, I just want to be your uncomplicated friend." That got me thinking. And I decided that is the kind of person I want to be: uncomplicated. You know, the kind of person who is exactly who you see. There is no hidden agenda, no hidden motive. There are no eggshells to walk on around me. Just uncomplicated.

Isn't it refreshing to be with someone like that? Someone with little or no emotional drama? It is so hard to be with the kind of people who make you think, *I am not sure who they are going to be today...*

I want to be an uncomplicated wife for my husband.

Not sure I always accomplish that, but it is certainly my plan.

I want to be the peaceful presence in his life.

I don't want to be a problem he has to solve.

Philip and I certainly have our issues to deal with, but I have decided that I don't want to carry the issues all day and have a funky attitude while we are working them out.

There is a story in the Bible about three men. Shadrach, Meshach and Abednego loved God, and in spite of a new law in the country, would not bow to an idol. The king did not like their decision, and so they were thrown in a fire. Yet they did not get burned up in the fire. The king said he saw a fourth man in the furnace, a man who looked like the Son of God. He told the guards to let the three men out, and when they did, their clothes and hair weren't even singed and "there was no smell of fire on them" (Dan. 3:27, *NIV*).

I love that picture.

I wonder how many of us could go through challenging times and not come out looking and smelling burned?

It's tough to be around a person who brings their past and all its shackles into every second of every day.

Let's be a little easier and more uncomplicated than that.

I think so much pressure would be relieved in relationships if we just decided to be happy with ourselves and our circumstances, no matter what they may be. There is no person on the planet that can make us happy; we just have to decide to be. Abraham Lincoln once said, "Most people are as happy as they make up their minds to be." I like that. It puts the responsibility in our own lap. Regardless of what is going on in the world, regardless of what is going on in our circumstances, we can control our attitude.

My son, Jordan, has spent some time in sub-Saharan Africa working to see that water wells are built in communities in dire need of fresh, clean water. After one of his trips, he shared this observation: In the midst of absolute, abject poverty, children were running around and laughing. Their circumstances were seemingly horrible. Many of their parents had died from AIDS. They lived in mud huts. They ate maybe once a day. They had no clean water.

Yet they were happy.

I am just thinking here, but most of us aren't in circumstances quite that dire . . . maybe we can choose to smile.

People sometimes say to me, "Holly, being happy is just your personality. It's easy for you." I don't think so. I roll out of the bed in the morning same as you. Like yours, my life is not perfect. I just make a decision. When I see Philip, am I going to put a smile on my face? When I go into the office, what kind of attitude is going with me?

Happiness is not a cloud that descends.

It is not a personality style.

It is a choice.

It is a decision to follow a certain path.

The *Amplified Version* of the Bible defines "blessed" as "happy, fortunate and to be envied." If we want to be happy, we must do the actions that produce it. As Americans, we are promised the rights to life, liberty and the *pursuit* of happiness. Some people have misinterpreted that to mean that we all deserve happiness. No, we don't. We only deserve the opportunity to pursue it.

We find happiness when we make conscious decisions to do what produces it. Let's take a look at a few of the paths that lead to happiness, according to the Bible. I encourage you to track down even more paths and get on them. Happiness is within your grasp.

"He who despises his neighbor sins [against God, his fel-lowman, and himself], but *happy* (blessed and fortunate) is he who is kind and merciful to the poor" (Prov. 14:21). *Want to be happy? Be kind and merciful to the poor.*

"*Happy* (blessed, fortunate, enviable) is the man who finds skillful and godly Wisdom, and the man who gets under-standing [drawing it forth from God's Word and life's ex-periences]" (Prov. 3:13). *Want to be happy? Find wisdom. Get understanding.*

"*Happy* (blessed, fortunate, prosperous, to be envied) are the people whose God is the Lord!" (Ps. 144:15). *Want to be happy? Let God be your God.*

"Blessed (*happy*, fortunate, prosperous, and enviable) is the man who walks and lives not in the counsel of the ungodly [following their advice, their plans and purposes], nor stands [submissive and inactive] in the path where sinners walk, nor sits down [to relax and rest] where the scornful [and the mockers] gather" (Ps. 1:1). *Want to be happy? Be care-ful who you spend time with.*

"Blessed (*happy*, fortunate, to be envied) is he who has for-giveness of his transgression continually exercised upon him, whose sin is covered" (Ps. 32:1). *Want to be happy? Live every day knowing that you are forgiven.*

"Blessed (*happy*, fortunate, to be envied) are those who dwell in Your house and Your presence; they will be singing Your praises all the day long" (Ps. 84:4). *Want to be happy? Don't just attend church. Do life there.*

Water from Your Well

You and I have a huge role to play in creating the atmosphere of our home. Proverbs 5 basically instructs us to keep focused on our marriage. It includes a warning about being seduced away by the "sweet" words of someone else. Verse 15 challenges spouses to drink "waters from your own well."

Now, I am aware that most of us don't get our water from a well. We simply turn on a faucet. But in biblical times (as in many communities in developing nations today) water was scarce and wells were carefully guarded. I have learned, through our work building wells with Generosity Water, that you can't just stand beside a well and expect water to appear before you. You have to lower a bucket or prime the pump. You have to *do something* to bring the water up.

This Scripture is basically saying, "Hey, quit looking at other wells. Look at your own well! Do some work to get the water out of this well."

In contributing to the atmosphere of your home and relationship, how do you drink from your own well? What can you do, what can you say, that will bring fresh water into your home?

What can you do to create a good atmosphere?

How about making a decision to think good thoughts about your spouse, even on days when you want to think bad ones?

Another proverb tells us that as we think in our heart, so we are (see Prov. 23:7). What we think determines where we go. We contribute to our perception of the world, including our attitude toward and love and respect for our spouse, by how we think. We control the direction of our thoughts.

We are not puppets. We are not robots. We can control our thoughts.

Maybe not the first one, because sometimes we are bombarded with something from out of nowhere. But we can control where we let that thought go. The second thought is ours. We control it.

There have been times when Philip has or hasn't done something that totally annoyed me. Maybe he didn't do something that he said he would do. (Grr . . .) Maybe he got too busy, or he forgot or he just decided that he didn't want to do it.

I could get irritated or get my feelings hurt.

Or maybe someone at work said or did something that created more work for me. (Very annoying!) Things like that happen to all of us. But I have noticed that I can either nurse that feeling until it is magnified, or I can catch the thought and stop the avalanche of bad thoughts that only produce destruction.

I am not saying that we shouldn't talk about what is bothering us or discuss issues that are important. It's just that if I don't control the thoughts that come barreling through my mind, then the words that come out are not helpful.

And the apostle James tells us that if we can't keep a tight rein on our words, we deceive ourselves and our religion is worthless (see Jas. 1:26).

This is where liking ourselves comes into play. I have found that those who like themselves tend to be happier, which means they create a better atmosphere wherever they are. If what's happening in our heads and hearts is generally positive, our environment and relationships will reflect that.

If You Can't Say Something Nice . . .

People who like themselves tend to be freer with compliments. They are not worried that giving a compliment will take anything away from themselves, so they often look for something good to say about someone. There are other people who are critical and seem to find fault everywhere they look. The sad thing is that they often are even more critical of themselves. Not a fun way to be.

How are you at giving compliments to the people in your world? To your husband? Maybe you should ask him.

Someone who is comfortable in her own skin can laugh at herself. She doesn't take everything soooo seriously.

I choke on my own spit.

I have fallen off a stage in the middle of a teaching.

I have had wardrobe malfunctions while cameras were rolling.

I have said words that, while appropriate in one culture, are absolutely *not* in another.

I have misspelled words while Twittering to thousands of people. Embarrassing? Yes.

But do I take out that embarrassment on others? No.

I just laugh and wonder what will be next.

Go on the journey of loving yourself. It's the first step toward having great relationships: loving our neighbor as ourselves. Get rid of those voices in your head that cause jealousy, strife and insecurity. Read God's Word and let Him tell you what He thinks of you.

As we learn to love who we are in God, it will bring life and joy to every season of our lives. It will deepen and strengthen our marriage, our communities and ultimately our world.

For more on the importance of knowing and loving who you are, check out a short video from Philip and me at www.godchicks.com.

Just for the Men!

We have to love who we are in order to love someone else.

We all deal with insecurities, but women generally have lower opinions of themselves than men do. This can cause them to be overly needy and insecure. Not good.

We all have needs that must be expressed and met, and it's possible for this to happen without being needy.

Neediness demands. Having needs asks. We tend to fall into one of the following categories:

1. Independent (thinking we can or trying to do everything on our own)—not good, because we are designed to do life together

2. Dependent (fully relying on someone else as an infant would a mother)—not good, because God, not our spouse, is the only one who can be our all sufficiency

3. Interdependent (confident, yet mutually dependent)— good, because we are designed for reciprocal relationships that are rooted in God

The goal is interdependence.

Men can also be insecure, but it looks different than a woman's insecurity.

Insecure men tend to be negative and critical. They can't laugh at themselves and are often just mean or manipulative. The only way out of insecurity is to see yourself as God sees you. When you begin that journey, you bring strength, kindness and love to your relationship. Your GodChick is counting on you.

Notes

1. Dr. Laura Schlessinger, *The Proper Care and Feeding of Marriage* (New York: Harper Collins, 2007), p. 64.
2. "Without You," written by William D. Collins, Thomas Evans, Michael Gibbins, Peter Ham and J.C. Molland, performed by Mariah Carey. © Apple Publishers LTD, c/o Bughouse Music, Inc., Los Angeles, CA.

2

Victorious Secrets

(Philip)

In the name of God! The soldiers will fight and God will give the victory!
JOAN OF ARC

*But thanks be to God, who always leads us in triumphal procession in Christ
and through us spreads everywhere the fragrance of the knowledge of Him.*
2 CORINTHIANS 2:14, *NIV*

It was like any other morning for 13-year-old Bethany Hamilton. She
went for a morning surf with a friend one October day in 2003, on
Tunnels Beach in Kauai, Hawaii. It was around 7:30 A.M. Bethany was
lying sideways on her surfboard with her left arm dangling in the water when a 14-foot tiger shark attacked her, ripping off her left arm
just below the shoulder. If the shark had bitten two inches further in,
the attack would have been fatal.

Bethany lost almost 60 percent of her blood that morning.

Her friends helped paddle her back to shore, fashioned a tourni-
quet out of a surfboard leash and wrapped it around what was left of
her arm, then rushed her to Wilcox Memorial Hospital. Bethany's dad
was supposed to have knee surgery that morning, but she took his
place in the operating room. She then spent six more days in recovery
at the hospital.

Despite the trauma of the incident, Bethany was determined to
return to surfing. Just three weeks after the attack, she returned to
her board and went surfing again. Initially she used a custom-made
board, longer and slightly thicker than her pro-board, that made it
easier to paddle.

After teaching herself to surf with one arm, Bethany began surfing competitively once again. She is now back to using competitive performance short-boards again. In 2004, Bethany won an ESPY Award for "Best Comeback Athlete of the Year" and was presented with a special Courage Award at the Teen Choice Awards. In 2005, with one arm, Hamilton took first place in the NSSA National Championships, a goal she had been trying to achieve before the shark attack. In 2008, she began competing full-time on the ASP World Qualifying Series (WQS). In her first competition against many of the world's best women surfers, she finished third. The book *Soul Surfer: A True Story of Faith, Family, and Fighting to Get Back on the Board* tells Bethany's incredible story.[1]

Bethany has become a living symbol to many who are faced with unbelievable obstacles and an example of determination and courage to continue on. The hardest thing for her to "relearn" about surfing after the shark attack was how to stand up and position herself in the right place; and waiting for the wave and then catching it.

Sometimes the hardest thing about life is recovering from tragedies, storms and heartbreaks. The hardest thing is learning how to *stand up and position yourself*. It can be hard to wait for the next wave . . . and then to catch it.

I want you to position yourself to catch the next wave. It's coming. It's building up on the horizon. Get ready.

What do you dream about? What causes you to believe in the extraordinary? What vision or idea brings wonder to your life?

A young girl might say, "I want to be a doctor, a ballerina or a world-class athlete."

What about you? What would you say?

Is it your dream to start a business?

To get a degree?

To get married and have a family?

To travel to another country?

To put your children through school?

Do you dream of winning a championship, being a teacher, helping the poor and oppressed?

Yogi Berra, the Hall of Fame baseball player and manager who was known for off-the-wall sayings, once remarked, "The future is not what it used to be." While some people might laugh at Yogi's confusing statement, to the walking wounded his words are a reality.

I believe God wants to rewrite your history. He wants to restore your future.

His dream for you is still what it used to be.

So many women survive heartbreaking, life-altering experiences. Some rise above the tragedies, while others allow those painful circumstances to define the rest of their lives.

The grief of losing a loved one.

Financial loss.

Physical illness and pain.

Rejection and betrayal. These are all real battles.

Real battles.

Some overcome and others struggle onward. Some live with crisis-imposed limitations on their lives.

Some catch the next wave.

The capacity to love others and be loved ourselves can be significantly limited by the hidden impact of battle scars. These battle scars can hinder our ability to trust, to be honest or to accurately interpret our own feelings. A limp in even one of these three areas impacts relationships of every kind—family, friendships, work relationships . . . and especially marriage.

The Epidemic

Sadly, two common experiences have marked the souls of millions of women, leaving them unable to soar to the heights they were created to reach—unable to catch the next wave. The wounds left by these experiences lead some women never to trust again . . . and if they do, they feel unable to trust with all of their heart.

One experience is abandonment.

The second is abuse.

A woman who is attempting to overcome the scars of literal abandonment or the disfigurement of emotional desertion will have to be determined in her pursuit of freedom. She will need to demand a level of dedication from herself that could be difficult to achieve. It will require her to navigate through the dangerous waters of trust—dangerous, but important.

It is a heartbreaking experience to depend on someone who has promised to be with you and then watch that person fade away. How disappointing it is to need help and find that there is no one to respond! That person promised to support you and always be there for you—but then one day, that person is gone. Perhaps it was a boyfriend or husband who first "went away" emotionally, and that led to his physical absence. You were left to wonder, *What did I say? What did I neglect? Is there something wrong with me?*

Sometimes this dynamic, played out in romantic relationships, begins with an emotionally absent dad or a mother who walked away. The seed of abandonment is firmly planted, and unless it is removed from the roots, it springs up again and again.

The number of women who have been abused is shocking, whether sexually, physically or emotionally, by fathers, husbands or strangers.

A gift mishandled.

A treasure once untarnished, now scarred.

I think to myself, *Wait. Stop it. That's* my *daughter! Those are* our *sisters. She is somebody's little girl. My Father cares about each of these women.*

I can't imagine the pain some of you have experienced, but I know this to be true: It is urgent that you win this battle. It is essential that you rise again. Love deeper. Believe with greater faith.

It's still in you. It's right there behind the scar.

Jesus had a dramatic message for women, yet the radical statement He made to women about themselves often escapes readers of the Bible.

There is a story known by millions simply as "The Woman at the Well."[2]

A woman approached a well in the heat of the day. She was a woman in similar circumstances to many reading this book right now. She had been abandoned and abused.

She was there to draw her daily supply of water. All the other women of the city had come and gone—they arrived early in the day because it was cooler in the morning. A morning visit to the well was more reasonable, the social norm.

But this woman did not come in the early hours anymore.

Too many looks.

Too many knew her story.

She had endured enough. The last thing she wanted was more questions, more dismissals and more condescending whispers. Those suspicious eyes . . . those eyes of accusation.

But there was something different about this day. A man had come to the well and was resting. As the woman began to draw water, the man told her about some "water" that He possessed, water that would never run out or leave her thirsting.

If you knew the gift of God and who it is that asks you for a drink, you would have asked him and he would have given you living water . . . those who drink the water I give will never be thirsty again. It becomes a fresh, bubbling spring within them, giving them eternal life (John 4:14, NLT).

Rather than addressing the woman's need for physical water, Jesus was speaking to the need in her soul. He offered her hope; if she would take a drink of it, she would never thirst again.

"Please, sir," the woman said, "give me this water! Then I'll never be thirsty again, and I won't have to come here to get water" (John 4:15, NLT).

Can you hear the hint of sadness in her voice? Or is it desperation? *Please, sir . . . give me this water.*

Did she want this water because she was thirsty, or did she want it so that she would never have to come to this place again? Perhaps she imagined for a moment that all her shame could vanish. If she never had to draw water again, she would not have to be reminded of the pain. The well was the place where she was reminded of her losses, her failures and her mistakes. Here, she was reminded that her best days were behind her.

Jesus then revealed that He knew about her failed relationships. She had five husbands. Ouch. *Five.* And apparently she'd given up on the marriage thing, because now she was just living with a man. At least it was someone to provide for her, someone to touch her. Not the kind of touch she would prefer, but better than the touch of loneliness. Better than no touch at all. "To the hungry, even what is bitter tastes sweet" (Prov. 27:7).

When I first heard this story, I thought that this woman must be immoral or wild or . . . I don't know. That something must be wrong with her.

That was before I knew that, in those days, a woman could not just drop a man. Women could not divorce their husbands. Women were at the mercy of men. A woman needed a man to provide for her. A divorce or the death of a husband left a woman desolate—without income or support. She instantly became a number counted among the poor.

This woman was not necessarily an immoral woman; she was a woman who had been abandoned. Five times.

Jesus touched her wound.

And of course there's the abuse. Married and dropped. Married and discarded. Married and thrust aside. Promised to and abandoned.

Not me, honey. I'm not like the others.

She'd heard that before.

What's worse . . . physical abuse or emotional abuse, sexual abuse or mental abuse? Abuse is abuse. It scars.

If you have experienced abandonment or abuse, I am so sorry. I am sorry that you have been treated this way. I probably don't know you. We have probably never met. But if I could look you in the eyes, I would tell you that I wish you had never been exposed to that hurt. If I could, I would make all the pain leave you. I would try to make the painful memories of your soul vanish.

You never should have experienced that hurt. I wish you were spared this violation. As a man, representing other men who may have hurt you, I want to apologize to you.

I am so sorry that you had to drink that bitter drink. There is another liquid being offered to you today. Drink.

This very minute, a miracle can occur in your soul. Today, we pray. We ask God to take away the heaviness, the hurts and the fears. Today we drink.

I don't have the power to heal, but there *is* healing for you. There *is* hope.

Jesus has this water. . . . If you could drink some, it would bring healing. There is healing and relief offered by the love of Jesus Christ.

Openly Worship Your God

I want you to know that you are going to be okay. You are going to get through this and God is still going to use your life to make a difference.

The Old Testament prophet Isaiah sometimes spoke to God's people collectively as if they were one woman in despair. I wonder if, through the prophet's words, the voice of the Holy Spirit might speak to you. A voice of hope. I believe He wants to speak to your heart. Listen as you read these verses.

"Sing, O barren woman, you who never bore a child; burst into song, shout for joy, you who were never in labor; because more are the children of the desolate woman than of her who has a husband" says the LORD. "Enlarge the place of your tent, stretch your tent curtains wide, do not hold back; lengthen your cords, strengthen your stakes. For you will spread out to the right and to the left; your descendants will dispossess nations and settle in their desolate cities. Do not be afraid; you will not suffer shame. Do not fear disgrace; you will not be humiliated. You will forget the shame of your youth and remember no more the reproach of your widowhood. For your Maker is your husband—the LORD Almighty is his name—the Holy One of Israel is your Redeemer; he is called the God of all the earth" (Isa. 54:1-5, *NIV*).

Can you hear His voice in these verses? Read it again. Listen harder. It's there. It's a whisper, but it's for you. Listen until the message sings loudly in your soul.

Sing for joy. Sing in celebration. Sing a song of worship.

The best example of how to worship God was revealed by a woman in a striking display of leadership. Jesus declared that her example should be told throughout the world. No higher standard has been established.

While he was in Bethany, reclining at the table in the home of a man known as Simon the Leper, a woman came with an alabaster jar of very expensive perfume, made of pure nard. She broke the jar and poured the perfume on his head. Some of those present were saying indignantly to one another, "Why this waste of perfume? It could have been sold for more than a year's wages and the money given to the poor." And they rebuked her harshly.

"Leave her alone," said Jesus. "Why are you bothering her? She has done a beautiful thing to me. The poor you will always have with you, and you can help them any time you want. But you will not always have me. She did what she could. She poured perfume on my body beforehand to prepare for my burial. I tell you the truth, wherever the gospel is preached throughout the world, what she has done will also be told, in memory of her" (Mark 14:3-9, *NIV*).

Worship that honors God and catches the attention of angels is worship that costs us something. It's not convenient. It is not easy. For this woman, it cost a year's wage. Her worship came from a deep place in her soul. It elicited criticism from others who had been offering a simpler, easier version of worship. Perhaps their style was more of a performance than an expression of passion.

But her worship declared to everyone that she had been touched by God. It was a response to the forgiveness she had embraced in accepting Jesus as her Savior, her Healer and her Redeemer. Her worship was displayed without reservation.

It captured the heart of Jesus Himself.

This kind of worship launches us into the deeper waters of healing.

Healing waters allow us to say with conviction, "You intended to harm me, but God intended it for good" (Gen. 50:20, *NIV*).

Worship gives us power to forgive and to pray, "Create in me a pure heart, O God, and renew a steadfast spirit within me" (Ps. 51:10, *NIV*).

To the woman who is not seeing the fruit of her efforts bring the results she hoped for—sing! To you who are not experiencing the momentum you dreamed you would—sing! To the one who thinks her future has passed her by—sing!

Sing! Worship, because God wants to get involved in your life.

I wonder if the woman who anointed Jesus was barren like the woman in Isaiah's word picture. Being barren in various areas of life has a tendency to paint a picture in your heart of what you can expect from your life: *No fruit. All hope, no results.* But the drink God offers and your response of worship can repaint the picture in your heart. God is saying, "I want to give you a new picture. It's a bigger picture, a better picture. It's brilliant! It's HD (Heaven's Definition)!"

Enlarge the place of your dwelling. Broaden the borders of your dreams—and this time, dream God's dream for your life. Fear not, it's time to believe again.

"Trust Me," God says. "You'll be glad you did."

Victorious Secrets

Healing is a journey.

It's an adventure.

It may not sound exciting at first, but it's necessary. You can do it. I believe that you can make it.

I've witnessed many people make this journey. As I've walked with them along the way, I've uncovered some secrets you need to know—the secrets for victory. The first Victorious Secret is:

1. Pursue a Present and Life-Giving Relationship with Jesus

Jesus offers us a *relationship*. This is so different than a religion. You may have embraced a religion that includes faith in Jesus. This can be a good thing, but it's not *the* thing. The main thing Jesus offers is connection.

To travel on this healing journey, it is crucial that you get connected to Jesus. If you once had a faith that produced this kind of life but now you feel disconnected, now is the time to reconnect. Connection begins when you open your heart to Him by praying something like this:

> *Jesus, I am going to trust You the best way I know how.*
> *I'm going to begin to follow You today. I need You to lead me.*
> *I need You to guide me. I open my wounded heart to You.*
> *Fill me, Lord Jesus, with Your healing presence.*
> *Show me how to drink Your living water.*

Jesus told the woman at the well that some people prefer to worship in the mountains and some in Jerusalem, but the Father wants us to worship in spirit and truth. In other words, we must engage. Engagement is the issue. To remain present in relationship is to engage, to participate with or become involved in. It's time to engage your faith. You can look from the outside in or you can get engaged. Pursue a present and life-giving relationship with Jesus.

The broken soul in us says, *I am scared to engage ... I don't know if I can do this.* Let me encourage you: You do not need great faith to survive. You just need little faith in a great God. You will not only survive, you will flourish. You will dance!

Isaiah told the barren woman to sing and shout for joy.

There must be a dance in there somewhere!

It's a dance of faith. A dance of life.

It's a dance of celebration.

It's a dance that allows you to disregard the circumstances—not to ignore them, but to rise above them. Dance in the face of former limitations. Look into the eyes of accusation . . . and *dance*.

This kind of celebration catapults you out of the past's questions and the future's distractions, and brings you into the present. *Why did this happen? How could he do this to me?* Some questions may never be answered, while the most powerful questions create a present faith.

Jesus attended a funeral where there were hearts full of sorrow and eyes filled with tears. One woman, who was suffering a lot, came to Jesus because she knew Him well. They had spent time together. They were friends. He loved her. She asked questions similar to the ones we want to have answered: *Why did this happen? Where were You?*

> When Martha heard that Jesus was coming, she went to meet Him, while Mary remained sitting in the house. Martha then said to Jesus, "Master, if You had been here, my brother would not have died. And even now I know that whatever You ask from God, He will grant it to You." Jesus said to her, "Your brother shall rise again." Martha replied, "I know that he will rise again in the resurrection at the last day" (John 11:20-24).

Notice that, at first, Martha was focused on the past ("if You had been here"). Then she switched her attention to the future ("he will rise again . . . at the last day"). But Jesus challenged her thinking. He took her out of the past, out of the future and brought her into the present. He brought her into the moment.

> Jesus said to her, "I am the resurrection and the life. He who believes in me will live, even though he dies; and whoever lives and believes in me will never die. Do you believe this?" (John 11:25-26).

I *am*.

Faith in Jesus needs to be present. This moment, called *now*.

I *am* the resurrection and the life, not I *will be* the resurrection.

Do you believe this? Can you believe? Can you stop focusing on the past and worrying about tomorrow and believe Him . . . now?

The apostle Paul wrote, "I tell you, *now* is the time of God's favor, *now* is the day of salvation" (2 Cor. 6:2, *NIV*).

The first secret of victory is pursuing a present and life-giving faith—today.

The second Victorious Secret is:

2. Embrace the Unconditional Love of God

God loves you, just as you are.

Whether you are broken or as strong as you have ever been, He loves you. His love doesn't go away. It remains. This is divine love, a higher kind of love than we are used to. There is nothing you can do to be loved less by Him.

Drink in His love for you. He accepts you. He embraces you. He adores you. He brings forgiveness to your heart. When you accept His love, you are free from your mistakes, your transgressions and your failures.

When you embrace His forgiveness for you, you can move toward experiencing that same forgiveness for others. (You may not be ready to forgive those who have hurt you; that may come later in the journey for you. It's up ahead a bit further.) Forgiveness is not something we can do on our own; His love empowers us to forgive. We do not release others from accountability by forgiving them; we free ourselves from the burden of bitterness.

Remember Isaiah's words: "Do not fear disgrace; you will not be humiliated. You will forget the shame of your youth and remember no more the reproach of your widowhood" (54:4, *NIV*).

The apostle John, known by many as the "apostle of love," wrote, "There is no room in love for fear. Well-formed love banishes fear. Since fear is crippling, a fearful life—fear of death, fear of judgment—is one not yet fully formed in love. We, though, are going to love—love and be loved. First we were loved, now we love. He loved us first" (1 John 4:18-19, *THE MESSAGE*). Embracing fearless, well-formed love is one of the secrets of victory.

The third Victorious Secret is:

3. Include Others on Your Journey to Freedom

James, the writer of the New Testament epistle named after him, has some great advice for us: "Confess your sins to each other and pray for each other so that you may be healed" (Jas. 5:16, *NLT*).

We need each other. That's how it works.

But trusting someone is tricky when you've been wounded by . . . trusting someone. When we're hurting, it makes sense to protect ourselves by building a wall around our heart. But that wall becomes our own prison, cutting us off from the people we need.

So we try again—and this time we hope to be smarter.

Sharing our fears and hurts with someone else frees us from our prison. Talking things through with a reliable friend relieves us from carrying the whole burden. Being transparent with a trustworthy partner helps us avoid deceiving ourselves.

Resist the urge to tell your story to the wrong people. This category includes those who are hurting so much themselves that they don't have a clear perspective, those who are too close to the situation, or those who repeat what you have said to others or react inappropriately.

In talking to the *right* someone, you discover a powerful element of the healing process. The right person might be a friend, a counselor, a therapist or a support group. He or she is someone who will listen to you, accept you, challenge you to keep on going on your journey, and will not talk to others about it.

As we reach out for travel companions on the journey toward freedom, we experience the truth of King Solomon's words:

Two people are better off than one, for they can help each other succeed. If one person falls, the other can reach out and help. But someone who falls alone is in real trouble (Eccles. 4:9-11, NLT).

The fourth Victorious Secret is:

4. Improve Your Serve

I had just had surgery. I needed to rest. The nurse entered my room and told me, "Let's get up and walk for a while."

What? "Did you read my chart? I just had surgery. I need to rest."

She kindly explained that *yesterday* is not the same as *just had*. "Walking is part of the recovery," she said.

"Great," I muttered under my breath.

You may still be reeling from wounds in your life and don't feel up to serving anybody. But the truth is that serving is part of the healing process.

Let's get up and walk for a while.

And while we're walking, let's serve people along the way. Jesus calls us to serve; it's what being a follower of Christ is all about. Serving touches others and it heals us. Improving your serve will build strength in your life.

> The greatest among you will be your servant. For whoever exalts himself will be humbled, and whoever humbles himself will be exalted (Matt. 23:11-12, *NIV*).

It was a very special woman who proclaimed, "I am the Lord's servant. . . . May it be to me as you have said" (Luke 1:38, *NIV*). When the angel visited Mary and told her that she would deliver God's Son in a few months' time, she could have resisted. She could have given a lot of reasons why she didn't want to go forward with God's plan. Instead, she called herself the Lord's servant.

Serving is the doorway to God's great blessings. He promised, "On my servants, both men and women, I will pour out my Spirit" (Acts 2:18, *NIV*). It is our experiences, both good and bad, that prepare us to impact our world. Could it be that the abuses you've suffered could become the platform from which you inspire others? What to others might be a tombstone could be to you a stepping stone that leads to a compelling future. This kind of victorious living starts with improving your serve.

The fifth Victorious Secret is:

5. Watch for the Wave

Here it comes! It's building. Do you see it?

> Now to Him who is able to do immeasurably more than all we ask or imagine, according to his power that is at work within us, to him be glory in the church and in Christ Jesus throughout all generations, for ever and ever! (Eph. 3:20-21, *NIV*).

God is able.
He is able to do more than you could dare to ask for.
He is able to do more than you could imagine.

There is a power at work inside you, like a baby squirming into the birth canal, preparing to enter the world. There is a seed that God planted in your soul, the seed of the dream He's had for you all along. No one can stop it . . . except you.
Rise up! Sing! Drink! Believe! Trust!
Love like you've never been hurt before.
You're invited into the dance of victory, which will release you into God's highest for your life.

Check out www.godchicks.com for more Victorious Secrets!

Just for the Men!

You have a mission. God is calling you.

There is an epidemic among women today. Perhaps a GodChick in your life has fallen prey to one or both of these two common experiences—experiences that wound her soul, scar her, lock her mind in the past, rob her of good relationships with us and attempt to disable her future:

Abandonment

Every woman knows the pain of abandonment. Even when a significant someone in her life has remained physically present, she knows the pain of his or her emotional withdrawal. She may have experienced abandonment with one or both parents, in an important friendship or mentorship, or with one of us—the men God called to protect and love her.

Abuse

Emotional, physical and sexual abuse are more common than any of us would like to admit. Neglect, name-calling, hitting, smacking or inappropriate sexual touch may have shaped her growing-up years. Perhaps she has accepted abuse because it is all she knows. She may secretly believe abuse is the only way she can be loved. She may have trouble believing that God's love is pure because she has so rarely experienced "love" that was not destructive.

Your mission is clear: Be a healer. If the woman in your world wonders about God's love, step up and be His example.

What if we decided to stand up in righteousness, to exemplify honorable character? Not only would women begin to understand their value, but they would also understand and trust the character of our God.

Abusers don't only destroy the lives of the women they abuse; they destroy their own lives as well—and they give the rest of us guys a terrible reputation to overcome! And men who walk out emotionally and/or physically on the women in their world abandon not only the purpose of those women, but their own as well.

We are called to lead. We need to lead in worship, in prayer, in honoring God and people, in our homes *and* in the way we care for women. You have a mission. God is calling you to lead the way. He wants to see His daughters healed, restored and protected by men who will rise up in the character of our Father.

Support her healing journey. Give her grace as she learns you are not her enemy. Lead her into the presence of God with both your words and your actions.

Notes
 1. Bethany Hamilton, Sheryl Berk, Rick Bundschuh, *Soul Surfer: A True Story of Faith, Family, and Fighting to Get Back on the Board* (New York: Pocket Books, 2004).
 2. The story is told in John 4.

3

I Wish I May,
I Wish I Might . . .
Have a Great Marriage
by Midnight!

(Holly)

Dreams do come true, if we only wish hard enough.
You can have anything in life if you will sacrifice everything else for it.
J. M. BARRIE

Through skillful and godly Wisdom is a house (a life, a home, a family) built,
and by understanding it is established [on a sound and good foundation].
PROVERBS 24:3

I loved Philip. He loved me.

Then we said, "I do."

And like Cinderella, I thought that was all it took: love and a wedding ring.

Cinderella lied.

Thinking that marriage is as simple as love and a wedding ring is about as naive as thinking that all you have to do to have great abs is to buy a cute workout outfit! Sadly, great abs come only after lots of crunches, Pilates and diet control.

Building relationships is a lot of work. Period. I don't know anyone who has been married very long who will not attest to that fact. Marriage requires a high level of commitment, loyalty and growth from the individual as well as the couple. Our character in our relationships determines the success of our relationships. So, when couples do the right kind of work—character work—more happiness and a deeper level of intimacy than they thought possible are discovered. But these always come as a result of hard work and going through some difficult moments.

And what are some of those difficult moments? Conflicts, fears, old traumas, big and small rejections, arguments and hurt feelings . . . the disillusionment of someone being different than we had imagined. All of these things are normal, and all of these things are workable. And if people work through them, they reach happiness again, usually a happiness of a deeper and better sort. They just have to do the work.

A counselor relays this story:

I was talking to a young man one day about his girlfriend. He was thinking about getting married, and he had questions about their relationship. Several times during the conversation, he said that something she did or something about the relationship did not "make him happy." It was clear that this was a theme for him. She was not "making him happy."

When I asked, I found that she wanted him to deal with some things in the relationship. He needed to do some work that took effort. It was not a "happy" time. When he had to work on the relationship, he no longer liked it.

At first, I was trying to understand what the difficulties were, but the more I listened, the more I saw that *he* was the difficulty. His attitude was, "If I am not happy, something bad must be happening." And his immediate conclusion was always that the "bad" was in someone else, not him. From his perspective, he was not part of any problem, much less part of the solution. Finally I had heard about as much as I could take of his self-centered ramblings.

"I think I know what you should do."

"What?" he asked.

"Get a goldfish."

Looking at me as if I were a little crazy, he asked, "What are you talking about?"

"It sounds to me like that is about the highest level of relationship you are ready for. Forget the marriage thing."

"What do you mean by the highest level of relationship?"

"Well even a dog makes demands on you . . . [A dog has to be] let out to go to the bathroom. You have to clean up after it. Other times, it requires time from you when you don't want to give it. A dog might interfere with your happiness. Better get a goldfish. A goldfish doesn't ask for much. But a woman is completely out of the question."[1]

Sort of funny . . . right?

Fairy Tales

Great marriages are not genetic. They don't happen just because you want one. If they did, everyone everywhere would have a great marriage.

Having the desire for a healthy marriage is really only the first step in a long list of steps. And sadly, many couples don't make it past the first few steps. Desire alone will not build a great marriage; in fact, desire internalized and unfulfilled will destroy a partnership.

But it's good to remember that struggling marriages don't "just happen" either.

On July 29, 1981, one of the most highly publicized and glamorous weddings in history took place. Great Britain's Prince Charles married Lady Diana Spencer. I remember watching it in the middle of the night . . . sighing . . . dreaming . . . loving all the regalia . . . and hoping my future husband wouldn't have ears like that!

An estimated audience of 750 million people worldwide watched the event. There were 4,500 pots of fresh flowers lining the route to St. Paul's cathedral, where 2,700 people crowded the grand church. More than 75 technicians with 21 cameras worked to enable the world to watch the ceremony.[2]

For many of us, this was a modern fairy tale. A royal prince weds a lovely lady in a grand cathedral surrounded by adoring subjects. Being rich, young and beautiful (well, *she* was!), they were the envy of millions. It seemed to be the perfect match. But if you've been around the block a few times, then you know things are not always what they seem.

And sadly, we know how that particular fairy tale ended. The couple grew apart, and the storybook marriage we all wanted to believe in eventually collapsed into adultery and divorce.

It takes more than a prince, a lady and a palace to make a happy marriage. For marriages to survive, they require regular maintenance. They require effort.

Right now, if you are thinking, *This is too hard. I must have married the wrong man,* then you are not alone. We have all thought that at one time or another. But he is probably *not* the wrong man; you just have some work to do. Good times are ahead!

Preparing to Be a Learner

Many people think that monstrous, miracle-like events are needed to change their marriage. That is not the case. I believe that it takes small tweaks to move the relationship to higher peaks.

I think it's the seemingly insignificant moments in life that determine both our relational success and our character. I know you don't feel like moving the kids' art project, the mail or your purse from the kitchen counter—but you know that the clutter irritates him, so love says you have to. He would probably love for you to speak to him in bullet points, but you wouldn't feel very loved if that's all he wanted, would you?

Patience, generosity, understanding, affection, quality time and care all come so easily in the initial phase of a relationship. He lets us share all the details. We think it's so cute that he can't find his car keys. He opens every door for us. We dote on his every word, admiration beaming from our faces . . . these are the ordinary expressions of love that make relationships extraordinary.

In the beginning, it all comes so naturally that neither of us can imagine ever getting irritated, hiding feelings or growing apart; but it happens. And it doesn't happen "suddenly," with one major incident, as we might think. It happens in the culmination of all the little things: junk on the counter, a pressing feeling to "get to the point" that shuts us down, continual arguing over the missing keys. And then there are unspoken hurts, frustrations, irritations, hidden agendas, false expectations, unexpressed dreams . . . tell-tale signs of an unlooked-after heart that is constantly tempted to wander.

There are a lot of reasons for divorce.

Communication breakdown.

Personality differences.

Sexual frustration or unfaithfulness.

Money problems.

Unresolved issues of the past.

But maybe at the core of all of these is just a lack of preparation. Most of us spend more time planning for the wedding than we do for the marriage.

And let's be realistic: It can't just be our spouse that is the problem (though there are days when I am convinced he is). Sometimes we might think that if we were just married to someone else, then our problems would be solved.

I don't think so.

I heard a celebrity interviewed several years ago, just after her second marriage. The interviewer asked, "How did you know this was the right one?" The celebrity just smiled and said, "When you know, you just know . . . there is this feeling." The last time I checked, she was on her fourth marriage.

Maybe her method does not work.

One out of every two marriages ends in divorce. That is *50 percent*. Can you imagine if you went to a bungee jump and the man operating the bungee jump said, "Come on, it's great! Two out of four people come back alive. Two out of four crash at the bottom, but wow, the fall is awesome! It is exhilarating. The anticipation is amazing. It gets your heart going . . . and, hey, we can make it a special thing if you want to bungee jump together. We can order flowers, have your friends wear tuxedos, and videotape the whole thing. Maybe you come back and maybe you don't. But we'll have pictures for your whole family."

Who is going to do that bungee jump? Not many people.

And yet we jump into marriage. We jump into relationships that have a significantly lower percentage for success and we say, "I know what I am doing! I am following my *feelings*!"

Sixty percent of second marriages end in divorce.[3] Some estimates indicate that 80 percent of third marriages can end in divorce and that up to 90 percent of fourth marriages end in divorce.

Maybe we have a few things to learn.

We all expect our physicians to go through years of school and residency in order to be good at what they do, yet most of us expect to have a strong marriage without ever learning how. Wouldn't it be great if all universities required all students to take Marriage 101? In the long run, that class would have proved more useful than the calculus class I took.

But for those of us who missed Marriage 101, there is hope!

We all need to remain a student in our marriage, continuing to learn and grow. Why is it that we expect to spend time and effort becoming better at our job or career, which may or may not last a decade, yet we neglect to acquire new skills and knowledge about our marriage? I am committed to being Philip's wife until one or both of us meet Jesus—that could be a *long* time (not as long as it was 25 years ago, but still quite a while!); shouldn't I get better at it as I go? Being his wife is a role I will have for lots of years, so I continue to learn.

Good for you for picking up this book. That means that you want to learn and continue to develop your marriage.

Sadly, most people don't.

I want to encourage you to keep at it. Philip and I have read hundreds of books about relationships. Books about how to talk to each other. Books about what his needs are and what my needs are. Books about why he is from Mars and is like a waffle, and why I am from Venus and am like spaghetti. We have listened to countless hours of teaching on the subject and we have attended many seminars together . . . all because we are committed to being the best at this marriage thing as we can be.

I tell singles that the number-one question to ask themselves about a potential spouse is, *Is this person a learner?* Because if someone is a learner, they will learn to be a great husband, wife, parent, employee . . . whatever.

I learned in biology class that the way to tell a living organism from a non-living object is by observing any change. If there is no growth or change after a time, the object is considered inanimate. Dead.

It is the same with you and me as individuals and as part of a marriage.

We must grow. As individuals and as part of a couple.

As individuals, we must be willing to learn new things and think new thoughts. By thinking old thoughts, we won't make it through life the way we are supposed to. We need to meet new people, read new books, take new challenges and set new goals. Basically, we need to be lifelong students. A few years ago I heard about a group of nuns who consistently lived to be more than 100 years of age. Wow! Some scientists went to their convent to study these sisters and see what was different about how they lived. Certainly their lives were more organic and pure, but the scientists also discovered something else. They got permission to perform autopsies on the nuns who had died, and those exams revealed that the brains of the nuns had many more connections between various points than most people's brains. These connections are formed when the brain learns something new. The scientists then discovered, after interviewing some of the nuns, that the group was committed to learning new things, right up until death. They were reading new books and learning to speak new languages all the way into their nineties. Because their brains were continually growing and being used, the nuns lived longer.[4]

You and I need to be people who want to learn new things—not only so that our lives will be longer, but also that they will be fuller. The growth that I make and the changes I embrace won't change who I am, but they will make me a better me.

Pienso que esto es una bueno idea.
Je pense que c'est une bonne idée.
Ich denke, dass dieses eine gute Idee ist.
σκέφτομαι ότι αυτό είναι μια καλή ιδέα.
Iay inkthay isthay isay ay oodgay eaiday.

(I just thought that I would help you with some of those brain connections!)

Most of us *say* that we want to learn new things.

And we probably do.

But saying it is easier than the actual learning. Once we realize how hard it is to do something new, it's very tempting to quit. But that's exactly what we can't do. We have to push through the learning curve.

My daughter is 18 and has spent years playing basketball. Thanks to her big brother, she has been dribbling a ball since she was a toddler. And after many seasons, she's a pretty good player. A few years ago I asked her to give volleyball a try, and she did. But after one season, she was ready to quit. She realized that she would have to work very hard to get good at this sport. It was new for her, and she wasn't willing to push through the learning curve.

Quitting volleyball is not such a big deal.

Quitting on a marriage is. Quitting on trying to understand each other is.

We each have to push through the learning curve in our relationships. In life and in relationships, there are lots of learning curves.

As part of a marriage, I've had to grow in a few ways. I've had to truly become a student of Philip—not only in learning his personality strengths and weaknesses, but also in learning his likes, dislikes and needs. From knowing the simple to the more complex—his favorite food to what he needs when he is hurting—and then being willing for him to change his mind . . . which means I have to learn new stuff all over again!

The tricky thing for me, early on, was learning about him *not* to change him, but to *know* him.

Some people come crying to a counselor, "He is not the person I married!" Well, probably not. And neither are you. Our tastes, interests and emotional needs will change. That's what keeps it interesting, and why we have to continue being a student.

For years—23 years of married life, to be exact—Philip did not like pasta. I think his mom fed him too much boxed macaroni and cheese as a child; when he thinks of pasta, he pictures boxed childhood meals. I thought this was just a bit weird. How could a person not like pasta? He likes rice, and really, what is the big difference? They both taste like whatever sauce you put on them. For years, I tried to convince him that not liking pasta was just wrong. I tried all sorts of recipes to entice him. Nothing worked. He did not like pasta.

My problem was that, rather than being a good student of my spouse in order to know him, I was trying to change him. Not good.

But now something even weirder than not liking pasta has happened.

Philip has decided that he likes pasta. I have no idea what happened. All I know is that now he is the one making reservations at Italian restaurants.

As a woman committed to being a student of my spouse, I am just trying to keep up!

He needs time to process most things.

He likes the computer and television on when he is studying.

He doesn't like human interruptions when he is studying.

He doesn't really like surprises.

He takes his time when making decisions.

He doesn't like interjections when he is talking. (He calls it "interrupting.")

He loves learning things by watching a DVD.

He reads multiple books at the same time, not always finishing any of them.

The first thing he wants to do in the morning is turn on his computer.

He doesn't like long meals in fancy restaurants.

He enjoys walking at a leisurely pace.

And I am completely the opposite in every one of those . . . which can make marriage challenging! Because sometimes, deep in my heart, I wish Philip was more like me.

This is not good! It means that I have stopped studying who he is and instead am focused on who I want him to be.

I mentioned that Philip does not really like surprises. I found this out the hard way. (Well, honestly I knew he didn't like surprises; I just thought he was wrong. Who needs to know every detail about what is coming?) One day, in the first few years of our marriage, I called his assistant at the office and let her know that I was coming to kidnap Philip for a few days, so she needed to cancel any appointments. I packed his overnight bag and made all the arrangements; we were just going to be gone overnight, so it was an easy thing to do. I got to the office and asked him to get in the car . . . and off we went! He was not nearly as excited as I was. In fact, he was just a bit irritated. He wanted to know where we were going and what we were going to do. And I was equally as irritated that I had to blow my surprise and give him all the details!

Looking back—and hindsight is indeed 20/20—he would have been much happier if I would have said, "Honey, how about if we go away for a night to Santa Barbara?"

Lesson learned.

Sometimes the differences in personality and preferences can be annoying. But I have found that where I am weak, he is strong—

and vice versa. We are attracted to each other because of the differences, and while they are often hard to work through, they make our relationship stronger. More on that in chapters to follow . . .

Ask Questions

Questions are a great way to learn about someone.

When Philip and I first started dating, he constantly asked me questions. Almost every time we were in the car, he asked me something.

It was great, because it meant that I was dating a man who wanted to get intimate with me by knowing my thoughts, my fears and my dreams. He was interested in the workings of my heart. How could I not fall in love with someone like that?

How about you? Are you asking questions?

Try these:

- What is your biggest fear?
- What do you want our life to look like in 5 years?
- If you had a million dollars, what would you do with it?
- What are two things you love about me?
- If money were no object, where would you like to go on vacation?
- What are you looking forward to?
- What makes you feel the most alive?

Over the years the questions might change—not to mention the answers!—but we should still be asking them. The truth is, both you and your husband are a mystery never completely solved.

A stale marriage occurs when no one cares enough to ask questions. When we quit learning about each other.

Dr. Robin Smith, in her book *Lies at the Altar*, suggests 276 questions that should be asked before marriage, and asked again during marriage. And they should be answered truthfully, not how you think your partner wants you to answer them. After all, it is truth that sets us free.

If you are dating and you don't have the time to ask the questions, then you don't have the time to get married.

Here are a few of the questions she suggests:

- Are you working in your chosen profession?
- How many hours a week do you work?
- Do you prefer urban, suburban or rural settings?
- Do you think of your home as a cocoon, or is your door always open?
- If you had unlimited resources, how would you live?
- Do you have any debts?
- When was the first time you felt that you were in love with another person?
- Do you exercise regularly?
- What do you like or dislike about your appearance?
- Do you want children?
- Have you ever been alienated from your family?
- Do you have a best friend?
- Are you serving in church?
- What is your idea of a fun day?
- Do you enjoy traveling?
- Do you like to cook? Eat?
- Are there household responsibilities that you think are primarily male or female?
- Are you a morning person or night person?[5]

Being a perpetual student is crucial. Not that you need to remain in college forever. Please don't. Learn and then do the work that is necessary. Continue to learn new things about life and about your spouse.

Wisdom for Life

Being a student and asking questions will produce knowledge. Knowledge is good. It is the first step toward gaining wisdom, and it takes wisdom to build a life, a home and a family (see Prov. 24:3). Wisdom is more than knowledge. It certainly requires knowledge about what is true, but it is coupled with knowing what to do. Wisdom comes from experience—your own or, for the smart ones out there, the experience of others. You don't need to stick your hand in the fire to know it is hot. It's enough to see the burn on the person who did.

Wisdom has a cost.

I have a lot of knowledge about cancer. I have read dozens of books and spoken to many health practitioners. I've also talked with women who have navigated their own journey and gained knowledge from them; in many cases, I learned what not to do.

What I did with that knowledge became wisdom. I have gained plenty of wisdom navigating my own journey. I've learned that how I eat, exercise and rest really do matter. And wisely, I changed. I eat, rest and exercise differently. Knowledge became wisdom because I acted on it.

Interestingly enough, some of the people in my world now eat, rest and exercise differently as well. They did not go through a cancer battle; they were just smart enough to learn from someone who did.

Wisdom builds a life.

Wisdom also builds a home and a family.

We can get knowledge from anyone. I can learn from someone who has been married 10 times. Mostly what I learn is what not to do. But that can also produce wisdom. Knowing what not to do is very good.

From a woman divorced two times: *We had very poor communication.*

From a man divorced one time: *We got married too young.*

From a woman divorced two times: *We didn't know how to handle conflict.*

From a woman divorced one time: *He wanted someone younger.* (After talking to her for a while, I realized that she was fairly bitter. She said that he had left her for someone who "thought he hung the moon." I guess he needed the encouragement she wasn't willing to give. While her husband was certainly responsible for his choices, somewhere along the way she had forgotten how important encouragement was to him.)

I remember recommending premarital counseling to a man who was newly engaged. His response was, "Why do I need that? I've been married four times before." Why indeed? Guess he was not that interested in the wisdom that can build a home.

Because I am a student on a quest to gain knowledge, which can then become wisdom to build my own house, I have done some research on why couples divorce. The results were interesting to me.

Sharon Pittman wrote:

Divorce is one of the worst things a person can go through. It doesn't matter who is right, who is wrong, who is at fault, how much better one will be without the other or anything else. That may all be true, but in the quiet moments, it still hurts.

> Divorce for many women is not only about the loss of a spouse and marriage, but the loss of a dream. You know that dream. The one where two people fall in love, grow old together and live happily ever after. It's the having just one person to grow old with, raise a family and build a life.
> Divorce takes a huge toll emotionally. Again, cause doesn't matter. There are still feelings of failure and wishing things could have been done differently or not at all. Regrets and hurts take years to get over.[6]

It does not appear that only one factor contributes to a couple's decision to divorce, and there are a number of reasons why marriages fail.[7] The number-one reason given by divorced couples is a lack of communication or poor communication. The second most cited reason is marital conflicts and arguments. Third, many divorced couples say infidelity led to their divorce.

While these are the primary reasons cited for failed marriages, statistics show that there are several underlying factors that contribute to these trends. Those who get married in their mid- to late-20s are less likely to get divorced than those who marry at a younger age, and that this age group tends to be more satisfied in marriage than couples who marry later in life.

Education and income both play a role in divorce. Data shows that a married couple with a higher education and a higher income is less likely to divorce than a couple with lower education and lower income.

Reports suggest that between 40 percent and 85 percent of couples who lived together before getting married had their marriages end in divorce. Interesting isn't it? Most people live together thinking it will help their marriage.

About 25 percent of adults in the United States have been divorced at least once in their lifetime. Characteristics of individuals that have a higher probability of divorce include:

- younger age at time of marriage
- lower education
- children from a previous relationship
- cohabitation prior to marriage
- sexual activity prior to marriage

As Jon Gottman and Nan Silver note, "One of the saddest reasons a marriage dies is that neither spouse recognizes its value until it is too late. Only after the papers have been signed, the furniture divided, and separate apartments rented do the exes realize how much they really gave up when they gave up on each other. Too often a good marriage is taken for granted rather than given the respect and nurturing it deserves and desperately needs."[8]

Now, perhaps you are looking at those statistics and thinking that you are in trouble . . . because you were 22 years old when you got married, neither of you went to college, and he has a child from a previous relationship.

Relax.

Your marriage can be different because you are getting the tools necessary to navigate the marriage adventure. If you are committed to being a student—to learning about yourself and becoming emotionally healthy, to learning about marriage, your husband and life—you have a much greater chance of making it to old age with the husband you now have! And not only making it, but also loving him the whole way!

Recently, I started talking to people who have been married longer than my 25 years. I am on the quest to gain knowledge.

I learned a few things:

From a man married 44 years: *Hold hands often.*

From a woman married 32 years: *Sometimes it is better to keep quiet.*

From a man married 31 years: *Let her do most of the talking.* ☺

From a man married 42 years: *Leave the house when she is hosting a wedding shower for a friend. Too much girl noise.*

From a man married 33 years: *Patience.*

From a woman married 30 years: *Persevere through hard times.*

From a woman married 35 years: *Decide that this is the man you want to grow old with, and do whatever it takes.*

From a woman married 36 years: *Smile often.*

All of this knowledge will become wisdom if I actually *do* hold Philip's hand often . . . and occasionally be quiet . . . and persevere through tough moments . . . and smile a lot.

Sometimes it might seem as if marriage is too much work. Yes, it does require work, but the work is necessary to produce unity, peace and *fun*!

Before I began pastoring The Oasis with Philip, I was an actress in Los Angeles. I have worked on a number of films, and each one required a lot of work. A lot of time. A lot of hours (eye cream, coffee and inconvenience!). Yet the end result was not just days of work . . . but a movie.

The end result of your work—your learning and regular marriage maintenance—will be a great marriage!

So don't lose focus.

Perhaps we all have a little ADD. But don't get distracted from what you are trying to build. And when you do, refocus and get back to building a life with the one you love.

> So don't get tired of doing what is good. Don't get discouraged and give up, for we will reap a harvest of blessing at the appropriate time (Gal. 6:9, *NLT*).

For more ideas on things that build your marriage, check out some short videos from Philip and me at www.godchicks.com.

Just for the Men!

Don't give up.

Unlike many women, you probably already knew that Cinderella lied. Real love is not quite like the fairy tales. Even still, maybe you are just a bit surprised at how much work a marriage takes. Sometimes when life gets hard, you might be tempted to withdraw, or just play rather than do the work that is needed.

Please don't give up.

Randy Travis sings a song that asks, "With so much riding on the choice at hand, the spirit of a boy or the wisdom of a man?"[9]

Make the journey from a boy to a man.

A boy is a child. He is entirely focused on getting his needs met. This is not bad; this is just what children do. But when a male is 20 years old and still pouts, throws tantrums or slams doors because he is not getting his way, it's not good . . . in fact, it's a little absurd. I have seen grown men display all of these behaviors—and if they don't accomplish the desired results, then the guys play all day, abandoning responsibility and the work necessary for building relationships.

Being a man means realizing the world does not revolve around you. A boy is concerned with taking care of himself; a man not only takes care of himself but can also do it while taking care of others. A man is an entirely different person from a boy; he's not just a bigger boy. A man will do the work necessary to build a family. Wisdom builds a life, so gain all the wisdom and understanding you can get. Be a student of your wife again—like when you were dating. Ask her questions. What are her dreams and fears? Feelings of love often follow the "doing" of love. Start doing in spite of what you are feeling. And thanks for caring enough to read the "Just for the Men!" section. You are already a hero.

Notes

1. Henry Cloud and John Townsend, *Boundaries in Marriage* (Grand Rapids, MI: Zondervan, 1999), p. 109.
2. "Diana, Princess of Wales: Engagement and Wedding," from Wikipedia.org. http://en.wikipedia.org/wiki/Diana,_Princess_of_Wales#Engagement_and_wedding (accessed December 2009).
3. Maggie Scarf, "Remarriage Is More Fragile than First Marriage," PsychologyToday.com: The Bonus Years of Adulthood, January 12, 2009. http://www.psychologytoday.com/blog/the-bonus-years-adulthood/200901/remarriage-is-more-fragile-first-marriage (accessed December 2009).
4. John J. Ratey, MD, "The Nuns of Mankato: Regeneration," excerpted from *A User's Guide to the Brain: Perception, Attention, and the Four Theaters of the Brain* (New York: Vintage, 2002). http://www.enotalone.com/article/6232.html (accessed December 2009).
5. Dr. Robin Smith, *Lies at the Altar: The Truth About Great Marriages* (New York: Hyperion, 2004), pp. 159-183.
6. Sharon Pittman, "Divorce Hurts: What You Can Do to Avoid It," EzineArticles.com. http://ezinearticles.com/?Divorce-Hurts---What-You-Can-Do-to-Avoid-It&id=2690665 (accessed December 2009).
7. Robert Grazien, "Statistics of Divorce," EzineArticles.com. http://ezinearticles.com/?Statistics-of-Divorce&id=1468444 (accessed December 2009).
8. Jon Gottman and Nan Silver, *The Seven Principles for Making Marriage Work* (New York: Three Rivers Press, 2000), p. 4.
9. Bruce Trey Edwin and Burtnick Glenn, "Spirit of a Boy, Wisdom of a Man" (Los Angeles, CA: Scott Hendricks Corporation). All rights reserved.

4

The Precarious Practice
of Kissing Frogs

(Philip)

You have to kiss an awful lot of frogs before you find a prince.
GRAFFITI

Theories pass. The frog remains.
JEAN ROSTAND

I'd kiss a frog even if there were no promise of a Prince Charming
popping out of it. I love frogs.
CAMERON DIAZ

You can identify them by their fruit, that is, by the way they act.
Can you pick grapes from thorn bushes, or figs from thistles? A good tree
produces good fruit, and a bad tree produces bad fruit.
MATTHEW 7:16-17, NLT

There is an old story about a young princess who finds a talking frog. The frog tries to convince her that if she will kiss him, he will turn into a handsome prince and he will marry her; they will live happily ever after.

The princess faces this dilemma: What if the frog is just making the whole thing up? What if she takes the risk, kisses a slimy and disgusting frog and then . . . nothing happens? Then again, what if he's telling the truth? He could be the prince of her dreams!

I guess the purpose of telling a young lady that "you have to kiss some frogs before you find your prince" is to encourage her to keep trusting and opening her heart to people, even after she has experienced a broken heart. Yet acting on this advice, a woman will keep trusting men who are not good potential mates, hoping that if she "kisses" the next one with her kindness and grace, he will become the man she needs.

Could this idea be more wrong? Every one of us experiences some personality enhancement because of the positive impact of someone's love. But *total transformation*? That definitely has "fairy-tale myth" written all over it!

Fairy tales are odd. Even the story of Sleeping Beauty, for instance: Do you really want a guy who will kiss a girl whom he has never met—a girl in a coma? What kind of nut is this guy?

Stop kissing frogs! Aim higher!

I want to tell you what I'd tell my own daughter, who is 18 as I write this: "When it comes to men, aim high! Don't allow just anyone access to your heart." A father's heart goes up and down the emotional roller coaster at the thought of his daughter trusting men who are clearly "frogs" that will never be changed by even the most loving of kisses.

Every girl wants a knight in shining armor. Women want to be pursued, to be loved and to be the heart's desire of a mysterious knight. But a knight's armor has a metal flap over the face area, and before you marry him, open the flap to see who is really inside there! That's all I'm saying. You don't want to discover, after you commit yourself to him for life, that under his armor is a self-indulgent, self-focused, immature young boy—not the hero you were hoping for.

Don't compromise. You are amazing, and you deserve amazing. Don't let your emotions guide you in a relationship. Pay attention. Does he really love you or does he love the idea of having a girlfriend?

In matters of the heart, look for evidence. I'm convinced that some women spend more time and energy evaluating someone to hire as an employee than they spend evaluating someone they date. A casting director takes more time selecting the right person for a TV show than many women take selecting the right person to cast as "The Man Who Deserves Access to My Heart." Why does a woman who is intelligent and attractive, who possesses great character and ability, select a man who is not safe, is not going to treat her well and is not good "spouse material"? Other men can tell that the guy she's pursuing is dangerous. Some female friends don't really trust the man, but some encourage her to proceed. Many women take the leap with certain men because "he has so much potential." Here's what you have to realize: Everyone has potential. Most people—really, *most* people—do nothing about that potential. Please put more value on results or progress than on potential alone.

From a Father's Heart

In addition to our biological daughter, Holly and I also have a handful of "adopted daughters" who have attended our church for some time. We love and care deeply about all of them, and it's heartbreaking to watch women I consider daughters go down the destructive path of risky choices in men. Why can't they use the same insight, skill and confidence they use in work or ministry and apply those to issues of the heart? Why is it that some women pursue "bad boys" or are attracted to men who are clearly risky and have "dangerous" written all over their lives?

When Holly and I were celebrating our twenty-fourth anniversary, I thought about girls who, because they settle for a frog instead of waiting for a prince, may never get the opportunity to celebrate even their tenth anniversary. I sat down and wrote a letter to my daughter, who was 17 at the time. I wanted to give her some ideas that might help increase her chances at a fulfilling marriage.

January 12, 2009

Dear Paris,
Today is your mother's and my 24th anniversary.
Those are kind of rare these days. Many times, relationships just don't make for a marriage that will last that long. Sometimes people stay married that long, but they just kind of endure it and don't really enjoy it like they once did.
My wish for you is that you enjoy a loving relationship and have a marriage that will last.
After having been married 24 years and helping hundreds of others in their relationships, I believe it has a lot to

do with who you choose to give your heart to. A father wants the best in life for his daughter, and I'm no different.

You once said in a video message that when you got married, you wanted a man like me. You may not need someone like me (although I loved hearing that), but I do hope you end up choosing someone to give your heart to who will be a great match for you. As a dad, I would say to choose someone who is good enough for you, someone who is worthy of you. Ultimately, this is your choice . . . no one can make it for you. Others can only hope that you guard your heart above all else.

I've given similar advice to thousands of others but I thought I'd share it with you on this special day in a more personal way. My advice to you, as your daddy, is to find someone who is:

1. A Christ-follower. This should be the number-one thing.

I'm not talking about picking someone who says he is a Christian; we've met many people like that. I'm not talking about someone who knows a lot of Scripture or has been a church member; there are plenty of people who do those things who may not make a very good spouse.

I'm talking about a young man who has a genuine love for God.

Find someone whose faith inspires you to believe more and live with a higher focus, a person who wants to honor Jesus Christ in how he lives and in the choices he makes.

This kind of faith will cause the person you choose to look for direction from a Source beyond his own thoughts and feelings. He will be compelled to be a servant at times when others focus on themselves; he will forgive when others want to hold on to little disagreements; and he will try to trust God when others just do it their own way. He will look to God's Word for guidance and will be accountable to God for his choices.

I've seen some people compromise on this number-one quality and regret later because it affects so many other areas.

It has been so valuable to share a similar faith with your mom.

2. Respectful. A person who respects you will think about your feelings and desires before taking action and making decisions. He will make decisions that demonstrate that he genuinely honors you.

Respect changes everything about how we talk to each other, how we work through differences and how we arrive at our ultimate decisions.

He will respect God's plan for your life. He will never encourage you or support you in disregarding what's best for your life.

Respect causes us to be kind in a way that others are not. It affects how we speak about each other to others and how we approach life together.

3. Protective. This does not mean he is *defensive*. He is *protective*.

To me, this means he is considerate of you. In our world today, it's easy to be self-focused. When the pressure is on, we tend to take care of our own needs first. A person who is protective will think of you before himself.

He will protect you physically from harm and from his own desires that would put you at risk. To young people this includes pregnancy and disease, but it also means meeting your physical needs in everyday life.

He will protect you emotionally by stepping up in times when you may need that extra sensitivity.

He will protect you spiritually by keeping a watchful eye over temptations and distractions.

He will protect your relationships, conducting his relationship with you in a way that does not jeopardize the other relationships that are important to you. He will not be competitive or unnecessarily jealous, forcing you to choose him in order to feel more important.

Love inspires someone to care for others enough to protect them.

4. A Man with Vision. A person with vision has ambition with purpose. A person with vision has direction.

Some people may have goals, but vision takes you somewhere.

Most young boys have big dreams. Some young men have interesting ideas about ways to make money. But ultimately you will probably want a man that is focused on "making a life," not just "making a living," someone who wants to make a difference in the world.

Vision brings confidence, confidence brings strength and strength brings greater vision. (Confidence is a quality that brings so much to a relationship, because it allows us to deal with situations that come up by focusing on those situations alone—not on our own hidden needs that subtly affect every conversation.)

Well, these are a few important qualities. . . . Maybe you can tuck this note away somewhere and let it speak to your heart in the months and years ahead.

My wish for you is to enjoy love in its highest form.

Love,
Dad

I'm not sure how much my 17-year-old valued the letter at the time, but I hope she keeps it and pulls it out from time to time, to think about what I've said as she makes decisions about opening her heart.

Dr. Gordon Livingston writes:

The choices we make, choices on which our happiness largely depends, involve judgments about the people we encounter as we travel through life. Whom can we trust? Who will bring out the best in us? Who will betray us? Who will save us from ourselves? These judgments are important in direct proportion to the closeness of relationship. If we are deceived by a salesperson, we have lost only money. If we give our hearts to someone unworthy of the gift, we lose more than we can afford.[1]

The secret to finding love that will last is to clarify what you want and then to pass on every frog who does not fit that picture. Learn to say no. When you can't say no, you end up in a relationship that is okay but not great, or great in some ways and mediocre in others—what I like to call a "Better Than Nothing" relationship. But the BTN relation-ship really *isn't* better than nothing; it hacks away at your self-esteem and makes you question your judgment.

The best time to say no is the first moment you realize that the person does not fit the picture you and God drew together. This is easier to say than do—it requires faith in God and in your own in-sight—but saying no can also be empowering. It is a way of declaring that you won't settle for less than you deserve.

Falling in Love . . . and Other Red Flags

She sees him. He smiles at her. She feels that special feeling down deep. Their eyes meet once more. The feeling is deeper with each look, smile and giggle.

Wow . . . falling in love. What a great feeling.

My philosophy is this: *Anything you can fall into—like a ditch, a trap or love—can really hurt you. Especially a ditch! . . . and love.*

Our world is full of relationship tragedies, where the wheels come off altogether! Horrible choices, poor strategies, sad outcomes and desperate methods always produce dismal results. Without realizing it, women and men use the same pitiful approaches to love and rela-tionships over and over again, yet somehow expect different results.

We have to be smarter about love. Be love smart. Be smarter about the issues of the heart. King Solomon told us, "Guard your heart above all else because it determines the course of your life" (Prov. 4:23, *NIV*). Who or what we allow into our heart can shape the rest of our life.

Once in a while I like to fish. I'm not that skilled at fishing, but I have fun. Some people just love the whole experience—you know, the bait, the hunt, the anticipation and the theories. Even if they don't catch anything, they love the whole experience and can't wait to go back again.

I like catching fish. All the other stuff is fine, but catching fish is the main thing for me.

A guy once told me, "If you wanna catch a fish, you gotta think like a fish."

How do you do that? How do you think like a fish? How did some-one figure out that we have to think like a fish? How do you know what they're thinking, anyway?

One thing I'm pretty sure about is this: I don't think fish ever reflect on where their life is headed. I don't think fish are worried about their relationships. I'm fairly certain that salmon girls don't ever say to salmon guys, "I don't think you care as much about me as I do about you." I'm pretty sure that fish never say, "Do you just love me for my body—my scaly, slimy, sleek body—or do you love me for who I am inside?"

Have you ever thought about how dumb fish are? I mean, fishermen catch fish all the time with *fake food*. That's what fishing lures are: fake food. Lures look like the real thing, but they're not—and they work! After all these years, you'd think fish would notice that when their friends eat that kind of food, they go shooting into space and never come back. You'd think they might hesitate to eat after that. But fish still fall for the trick, even after all this time.

Aren't you glad that people, human beings like you and me, are smarter than fish? We don't fall for the lure. We learn from the mistakes of others.

Right?

Let's be honest: In the area of relationships, sometimes people are like fish. We do not learn from the mistakes of others. We miss the red flags and swallow the lure—hook, line and sinker.

Red flags are warning signs. Red flags mean "Slow down, danger ahead." Let's talk about some of the red flags of risky relationships.

Red Flag 1: Too Close, Too Soon

One big mistake people make is going too fast. Learn how to pace yourself; be careful not to get too involved quickly or to let your emotions go without restraint. Don't say too much too soon about the intimate desires of your heart. When you allow yourself to feel things too deeply and strongly before you know the person very well, you set yourself up for heartache. Don't allow him access to your heart before you know he can be trusted.

If you're the kind of person who tends to move too fast (or your friends tell you that you're the kind of person who moves too fast!), you are really not in the best position to be dating. Some people think that maturity is an age issue: "I'm old enough to date; I'm 16!" But it's really not a matter of age. Maturity is more a matter of the condition of your heart.

The Scriptures tell us that "it is not good to have zeal without knowledge, nor to be hasty and miss the way. A man's own folly ruins his life yet his heart rages against the Lord" (Prov. 19:2-3). Don't have so much zeal that you are hasty and miss the way of wisdom. Slow it down. Many people don't understand that a major point of dating is to evaluate the other person's character. Is he a good problem-solver? How does he handle conflicts? Is he respectful of others, even when he is going through stressful situations? Does he overreact and attack those close to him? Here is the fundamental question about his (and your) readiness for marriage: Is it possible for him (and you) to love another person as much as he loves himself (and you love yourself)?

Try to answer these questions—finding the answers is one of the main reasons for dating. Some think only about the excitement, the passion and the emotion of dating, but those are less important than the quest for answers . . . and that takes time.

I once heard Neil Clark Warren, founder of eHarmony, give a talk in which he cited a study from Kansas State University. This study revealed something interesting: Couples who dated for more than two years before marriage scored consistently high on a marital satisfaction scale. The risk of marital failure diminishes significantly with longer dating periods. Despite this undeniable evidence, many couples think, *But we're different. We love each other. We will beat the odds. We pray; we read the Bible. We have God on our side.* All of these elements are good, but time makes all of them more effective.

On top of taking too many emotional risks too soon, some people also get too familiar physically too early in their relationship. I'm not talking about having sex; I'm talking about the physical expression of intimacy in a social environment, and what it says to one another and to others—whether we realize it or not.

A young lady once said to me, "I'm considering this person, as a boyfriend. We've dated a couple of times. I'd like you to meet him and let me know what you think before I move forward." So, when we were all together in a social gathering, I looked across the room and I saw them. The way they were interacting physically—touching, hugging and holding each other—I thought, *You don't look like you are "considering" anything! Physically, you've said, "I'm yours, I'm holding nothing of my heart back from you."*

Let's say that you see a married man talking to a young attractive woman (not his wife) who is standing 12 inches in front of him. She's touching a button on his shirt, looking down and giggling, then looking up at him through fluttering lashes.

Would that seem appropriate to you? No! You'd think, *What is going on here?*

What is being said physically is too familiar, and it indicates an emotional attachment that is improper for two people who aren't married.

Even if the man was not married and the two were dating, that level of physical affection and familiarity may not be appropriate. I believe that someone should earn access to physical affection over a period of time.

Dr. Joyce Brothers reports that before marriage, the average American woman has kissed 79 men.[2] That is a lot of research! Are kisses really so insignificant that it's okay to hand them out to just anyone?

There are a few good reasons for taking it more slowly.

First, we can't get to really know a person over just a short period of time.

It's always a surprise when I find things out about people I've known for years. It's not that they were hiding something; that particular information has just never come up before.

"I served in the military and I fought in Iraq for six months."

"Really? Wow, tell me about that."

"I had this odd job once in Europe."

"Huh. You lived in Europe?"

"I know how that guy feels because I was arrested once when I was younger."

"What? I didn't know that . . . what happened?"

"My dad died of cancer when I was young."

"I knew you all this time and I didn't know."

This is new information. It doesn't hinder our friendship; it's just new information.

But you don't want to get information on your honeymoon that could significantly impact your marriage.

I was married twice before.

I've had an STD.

I spent time in prison.
I've been through bankruptcy.
I am a Red Sox fan.

"This would have been good information to have . . . yesterday!"
Married couples come in for counseling and say, "Everything was
fine for a couple of years and then all of a sudden he stopped doing
this or she started doing *that*." When I hear that, I know that some
kind of need has surfaced that was there all along. It's likely that,
given a bit more time before walking down the aisle, that need might
have been discovered and dealt with.

I've also heard so many explanations from couples seeking premarital counseling about why they don't need any more time—they
are the exception to the rule.

"I know God's leading me."

"I've never felt this way before."

"We talk on the phone for hours. We know everything about
each other."

And so on.

Getting to really know each other takes time. Is it worth risking
your heart and a rest-of-your-life relationship to skip three to six
months of evaluation?

The second good reason for taking a relationship slowly is that
we need time to bond adequately for marriage—and throwing physical affection in the mix confuses our emotions.

Hopefully, there are some pretty high emotions mixed into your
relationship. That is normal. But emotions can make it difficult for
you to evaluate whether marriage is the right choice. Is it possible
you have missed something? Ruling out that possibility is the benefit of pre-marriage counseling and taking time to get to know each
other better.

This brings us to another common problem: Many people do not
get out of a dead-end relationship early enough.

When we recognize that a dating relationship is not going to
grow long-term, it is wrong to keep going just because we don't have
the courage to admit it. We should have enough respect for the other
person to back out gracefully so that it doesn't become unnecessarily hurtful.

Many times people break up six months or even a year into a relationship—but if they were honest, they knew earlier that it wasn't going to work. They just didn't want to be alone or didn't want to hurt the other's feelings. But it's better to hurt someone's feelings after a few dates than after several months, when the emotions are deeper for both people. I can't remember the names of people who opted out with me after a date or two. I've never gone to therapy over their rejection. It's the relationships that ended after six months to a year that caused real heartbreak.

The Scriptures tell us that we should not defraud one another in this matter of relationships (see 1 Thess. 4:6). It's dishonest to let something continue on when we know that it does not have a future. If you're afraid of how the other person will react, isn't that further confirmation that you shouldn't have a future together? If you can't be honest with him or are afraid that he'll blow up, he is not the kind of person you want to engage in a life-long partnership with. Healthy partnership requires honest communication and the ability to grow and change with the seasons of life—together. And since time is something you can never get back, don't waste any more of yours or his by being dishonest.

The third reason for taking a relationship slowly is that, when you do, you protect yourself from getting attached too quickly.

Protect your heart. Proverbs says to guard your heart *above all else*.

Is that how you live your life? Is that your priority? Or is guarding your heart further down the list than . . .

Above all else, try to find somebody.

Above all else, don't be alone.

Above all else, get somebody to give you a call.

Make guarding your heart your number-one priority.

Can a relationship work if you get married after dating for two months? Yes, it can. It's possible. But there is no reason to put yourself in this risky situation, especially when the odds are stacked against you. Forever is a very long time, so what's the rush?

I'm asking you to consider waiting at least one year (two is even better!) before you get married. Get to know each other. Go through different seasons; go through various circumstances; go through good times and bad times together, because you want to be sure this is somebody you can trust.

Over time, you'll be able to distinguish the lure of pseudo-intimacy from the real thing. We all have a craving for human closeness. But that deep, satisfying connection can only be achieved over time with openness, honesty and shared experience. In a world of impersonal associations, it is easy to be deceived by experiences that have the look and feel of genuine intimacy, but are in fact fake. Pseudo-intimacy is primarily about self-gratification, while true intimacy grows when we are other-focused. Understanding the difference is the best guard against involvement with someone who cannot or will not share the deepest parts of himself.

Guard your heart.

Red Flag 2: Lack of Personal Growth

Dr. Gordon Livingston writes, "The romantic idea that we can fundamentally change another person with our love and support is a dream seldom realized. . . . The best guide we have to future behavior is past behavior."[3]

A commitment to personal growth is essential to relational success. I'm talking about personal *growth*—not personal survival, not personal enjoyment, not personal accomplishment. Personal growth.

Great people are dedicated to personal and spiritual growth. Personal growth happens when you recognize a lack in your life and decide to change it. You identify an area where you'd like to grow and begin to learn—you read a book, you attend a seminar, you take a class.

People who develop their thinking are interesting people. Holly has told me this is one of the qualities that attracted her to me. I've always been somebody who wants to grow in the way I think, in the way I feel, or in what I am learning. It's common knowledge that men do not read books on relationships. I do. Men don't read books on parenting. I do. I want to know. I want to grow. I want to learn. I don't ever want to think, *This is all I know about being a husband and father, so I hope it's good enough.*

Two people who are dedicated to personal growth are essential to a healthy relationship. Everyone has problems, and we must all work on those problem areas of our life, whether they are spiritual or emotional. Then, as we grow as individuals, we become confident in who we are and don't need to force our perspective or will on others.

We become flexible and adaptable, two qualities that smooth the rough patches that inevitably arise on the course of life.

Our celebrity-crazed culture is consumed with appearance. Billions of dollars are spent each year on diet pills, cosmetics, surgeries, personal trainers and the latest fad diets. We ought to put at least equal effort into developing our heart, soul and relationships as we put into our physical health and appearance. The payoff is even greater.

A physical trainer told me, "When you lift weights, you can't just do the same exercise all the time. You've got to confuse your muscles. You've got to change the exercise, or else your muscles kind of anticipate what you're going to do and find the easiest way to achieve it. You've got to confuse your muscles." This is easy for me. I just walk into a gym and lift one weight—my muscles are plenty confused. The point is that it takes time and effort to have an effective workout strategy. One kind of workout may work for a while, but then we need to change things a little. A person who really wants to reach the physical results will do what he or she needs to do. The same is true in the area of personal growth. A person who really wants to grow will continue to put effort into improving his or her attitude, motivation and character.

When you're in a relationship, you're the only one who can change. You are in charge of yourself. You can't afford to think, *If my spouse changes, then I'll change.* This is why it's so important to see clear evidence that the person to whom you trust your heart is someone who has a continual desire to grow. Growth will always be necessary in life, and growing will always be part of the solution to relationship issues. If your mate refuses to grow through the current circumstantial limitations, the depth of your relationship can come to a halt. When your mate digs his or her heels into the ground on any subject, you are left to prayer and just loving that person as he or she is.

If you're single, pursue confidence and contentment at this stage in your life. Don't wait, thinking that somebody else is the answer to your discontent and self-esteem issues: "I am unhappy now, but if I find someone and begin a relationship I'll feel better and be better." The person to whom you join your heart should be an incredible addition to your life—that's the benefit of a relationship—but you must take the initiative to grow whether you are in a relationship or not.

Someone once said to me, "Philip, pray for me . . . I'm single."
Being single is not a sickness from which you need to be healed.
You can be single, focused and fulfilled.
I hope you think, *I love my life. I like where I'm going. I'm content right
now.* Be careful about the insidious belief that a partner will bring
wholeness to you. Two incomplete lives can't make a whole; you must
both seek healing, wholeness and growth in God. Then, together, you
can accomplish amazing things.

A commitment to growing in heart and mind, whether you're single, dating or married, will allow you to live from greater strength,
interacting with people and handling situations without being para-
lyzed by neediness.

Red Flag 3: Too Many Incompatibilities

A strong relationship needs a foundation of similarities and common
connection. Holly and I often laugh about how different we are—the
standard differences between men and women, personality differences and differing levels of energy—but too many differences can
bury a relationship. We have learned to find value in our differences.
She brings strengths I don't have to our marriage. I bring strengths
she doesn't have to our marriage.

Having said all that, we don't underestimate the power of our
similarities in the most important areas of our relationship. Common values and interests allow couples to work through their differences, and it is what we have in common that make us so compatible.
C. E. Rollins, in his book *Are We Compatible?* writes that compatible
couples have a strong foundation of similarities in background, temperament, goals, dreams and values, and have similar ways of managing their mental and physical lives.[4]

To be honest with you, Holly and I have what I would call "irreconcilable differences." I will never think the way she thinks. I'll never have
the emotions and thoughts of a woman. She'll never think like a man.
But we've learned to love and respect each other and our unique approaches to life. Those irreconcilable differences are not going to break
up our relationship, because we also have some strong unified values.
We share a strong sense of vision and agree about the priorities in our
life. These priorities define us—family, ministry, fun and what contentment really means—and allow us to navigate through our differences.

Don't be careless and think that your differences don't matter very much. One day you'll hit the wall and wonder, *What are we going to do now? Maybe I married the wrong person.* You will need to know and trust that your core values are compatible, in spite of your differences. Areas of compatibility that can be crucial are:

Emotional compatibility
Physical compatibility
Compatible energy levels
Cultural similarity
Spiritual unity
Recreational enjoyment

Emotional Compatibility

This is about being in tune in the areas of needs, expectations, goals and dreams. Being in sync with each other about what brings a sense of contentment in life is important. These are the things that bring joy and satisfaction in life. Without emotional compatibility, one can be happy and the other discontent in the same set of circumstances.

Physical Compatibility

It's important to be physically attracted to each other, yet some people are tempted to ignore this aspect and over-spiritualize their relationship. They believe that because they share the same faith, that will be enough to sustain them. Faith *is* important, but physical chemistry is also significant. Yes, appearances will change over the years— some things will wrinkle and others will sag—but that fact doesn't diminish the value of a basic attraction between spouses.

Compatible Energy Levels

An older man who had been married to his wife for 50 years was sitting on the sofa. His wife yelled downstairs to him, "Honey, come upstairs and make love to me!" His first thought was, *I don't have the energy to do both.*

Holly and I have different temperaments. I have a more introverted personality and a lower energy level, and I'm eight years older than she is. When she wants to do more, I want to do less. When I want to go out, she wants to stay home. Sometimes when we go out to dinner, she has a glass of wine and I have a double latte, in hopes that this will bring our energy level to a similar level—we are hoping to meet somewhere in the middle. (It has never worked.)

In your relationship, one spouse may want an active vacation and the other may prefer a relaxing time of rejuvenation. Your husband may see adventure as the ideal way to enjoy a night together, while your desire is for a quiet evening, watching a movie at home. Energy and activities can be negotiated, but it's important to be aware of these differences.

Cultural Similarity

Your "culture" is the combination of your background, family heritage and growing-up experiences. We have many interracial couples in our church. It's a beautiful thing; we love it. But as pastors, we also aren't shy about reminding partners that their cultural differences may have to be worked out as time goes on. Some people are excited at first about the "exoticness" of being with someone of another race. Their partner was raised in another country on the other side of the world and it's exciting to be with someone so different—but that excitement doesn't change the fact that culture can be an influential component to harmony.

Even two people who are both white, brown or black can come from cultures different enough to create issues. Did your family open gifts on Christmas Eve or Christmas morning? Did your parents split up chores along gender lines? Does your family have expectations about how much time you will spend with them? Do you feel more at home in the city, in a suburb or in a rural area? All of these questions have to do with your cultural background, and you and your partner may have to negotiate the areas where you differ.

Spiritual Unity

Mutual faith is important and should be non-negotiable. In fact, the Bible tells us that we should not be "yoked together" with unbelievers (1 Cor. 6:14). This is referring to our faith, our spiritual perspective in life. There has to be unity, similarity and connection.

If you are an unbeliever and you're dating somebody who is a Christian, that person must care about you a lot, which is clearly evident by him or her pursuing a relationship with you. They are, in a very real way, jeopardizing the depth of their faith by including you in their life. The reality is that someone is going to change. I hope the one with less faith will increase their faith, but for over 25 years of ministry, I've noticed that usually the person with more faith lowers their intensity and passion for God to accommodate the person with little or no faith.

If you are an unbeliever and you are attracted to or in a relationship with somebody who is a believer, I encourage you to consider that it is their faith that makes them so attractive to you. I challenge you to consider making a decision to become a follower of Christ yourself. The person who means so much to you may be another one of God's ways of reaching you.

Genuine faith guides your life, so believers should be protective of their faith above all else. The Old Testament prophet Amos asked the pointed question, "Can two walk together, except they be agreed?" (Amos 3:3, *KJV*). Too many people end up with a kind of faith that's politically correct, yet empty: "I respect your faith; you respect mine." They don't want a Christian marriage; they want a peace treaty.

I've noticed an interesting version of faith in some dating relationships; I call it Faker's Faith. A faker goes through the faith motions in order to be close to the one who actually has faith. It's not necessarily sneaky, but it's not real. Men, especially, can change radically for a short period of time to impress a woman—some men even act like they love shopping for months and months! Other men display an interest in God while dating, only to let their pursuit of faith return to an insignificant level after marriage. There is a major difference between somebody who is willing to go to church and serve God just because it's important to his love interest, and someone who actually has a faith that guides his life. (And as a side note, this is another reason dating at least a year is a very good thing: It allows you to see the depth of his faith.)

Mother Teresa had a pretty simple mission. It was to love and comfort the sick and dying in Calcutta. Unfortunately, some people have unconsciously adopted a similar mission statement for dating and even marriage. She picks a partner who is spiritually or emotionally sick and dying, who is unable to pursue a long-term, intimate relationship because he cannot give back. One person is the nurse and the other is the patient—for the rest of their lives.

Don't make excuses for people. Love them. Respect their faith or their non-faith. But recognize that "evangelism dating" is dangerous to the heart. Think about it: Dating someone to evangelize him is a relationship based on a hidden agenda. "I'm going to act like I love you just like you are, but I secretly hope that you're going to have a faith like me. I'll take you to church and maybe you'll get saved, and then I'll fully love you." Does that seem a little dishonest to you? There's a hidden pressure coercing the other person. It's a spiritual audition. Do you want to build a relationship with somebody who has a secret agenda to change you?

Believers and non-believers aren't the only ones with differences; there can be spiritual incompatibilities even between Christians. Believers can differ when it comes to beliefs, doctrine, worship preferences and church type. Some believers put a major emphasis on missions in developing nations, while others are focused on local discipleship. Some like loud, energetic worship while others prefer a more reflective style.

If you disregard these kinds of differences and move forward in your relationship, you may find yourself in disharmony. When you come to a place where you're praying that God will intervene in your marriage, you realize your faith is pulling you apart rather than bringing you together.

The powerful truth is that faith can totally transform a relationship, but it has to have enough similarities. Spiritual unity will help you deal with the difficulties that come your way in life.

Recreational Enjoyment

What do you like to do for fun? When you are dating, your parameters for what you consider acceptable entertainment will be much wider than they will be after you get married. Life gets hard, and for this reason recreation and relaxation become crucial to your personal and relational health.

You do not have to enjoy everything your spouse likes to do for recreation, but there must be a few things that both of you enjoy doing together. For instance, I've always loved to ride horses. Holly and I have owned several different horses over the years. Holly has ridden with me many times in the past, but it just does not have the same impact for her that it does for me. So I ride with my kids or my friends, or even get away out on the trails by myself.

Many couples whom we've counseled find themselves with this kind of disconnect—and the relationship quickly dries up. This is why I say that you must find some things that you both enjoy doing *together*. Find some activities that are fun, interesting, engaging and valuable to both of you. These could include hobbies, sports, exercise, entertainment, or a particular skill. It could be reading, hiking, boating, ice skating, fishing, going to restaurants, playing cards or games—even playing ice hockey. It doesn't matter what it is, just as long as it builds companionship and recreation.

Red Flag 4: Emotional Recklessness

Emotions are a great impostor. Emotions are convincing. They can make you believe that relational red flags are simply not significant in your situation. Emotions can make you feel like you've heard the voice of God telling you to do something that the Bible would never support. An emotionally driven relationship feels first and thinks later . . . and it's headed for a train wreck.

Emotions tell you to ignore your brain in matters of the heart. When they are in charge, a miracle takes place; it's called "brain relocation." Your brain ceases to function from the seat of reason and moves from your head to your "gut." (And when sex is involved, the brain migrates even further south. We don't make the wisest choices when sexually aroused, because sexual passion is easily mistaken for emotional passion—which is, in turn, mistaken for good sense.)

Isaac Hayes used to sing a song called "(If Loving You Is Wrong) I Don't Want to Be Right." That is the perfect way to approach relationships. *Not!* One of the most important abilities you can develop for relationships is the ability to turn your back on your emotions long enough to make the right decision.

People don't usually get pregnant outside of marriage because they've thought everything through; it's usually because of a poor decision in the heat of the moment. It's an emotionally driven, sexually driven action that shapes the rest of their life.

Clear values and personal boundaries will help you navigate through emotionally intense situations. It's difficult to make a clearheaded decision about your sexual boundaries when your shirt is off and you're breathing hard. Deciding your boundaries in advance, when your emotions are not clouding your judgment, will help you live up to your values. (Keeping your shirt on while on a date is a great value to consider.)

A person driven by their values, rather than their emotions, tends to have more confidence in the face of the many circumstances life throws at them. They usually handle conflicts well, whereas an emotionally driven person does not. Emotions crowd out peace and escalate problems.

An emotional person pressures others and tries to manipulate them. An emotional man may pressure his date to have sex, and try to make her feel guilty if she refuses—as if she "owes" him something. An emotional woman, on the other hand, may pressure her boyfriend or husband to give her everything she wants, regardless of his ethics or boundaries. Emotions can weigh down the relationship and steal the life from it.

We want to be in love and to experience the wonderful feelings of romance. We should be able to enjoy the feelings of loving relationships . . . but we can't be led by those feelings.

There are two important safeguards against an emotionally driven relationship. The first is having mature, married friends who have the kind of marriage you want, to whom you can go for advice. (The counsel we take is extremely important in shaping our relationships; it's a mistake to seek advice from single friends or from friends who are living an emotionally driven life themselves. It is smart, however, to glean wisdom from a counselor or coach who can help you interpret your feelings and the circumstances you are facing.) Advice from mature, married friends helps you guard against an emotional recklessness because they have likely been tempted in similar ways. They can say, "I think you should slow it down; your emotions are taking over here" or "Hey, this is a red flag. You're not thinking this through."

The second safeguard against emotional recklessness is a clear list of your values. You may choose to write them down or just think them through, but once these values are established, you do not deviate from them. They are written in your heart. You talk about and deeply believe these values, and they guide you and shape your life.

Red Flag 5: The Absence of Service

When it comes to clothing, Holly does not see wrinkles. I'm not sure why.

"Holly, are you going out like that?"

"Yes, why?"

"Your dress is wrinkled."

"It's not that bad. No one can see it."

"Trust me on this one, they can see it. I'm a person and I can see it."

"It doesn't matter."

"Take it off; I'll iron it," I offer.

"You really think it needs ironing, or are you just trying to get my clothes off?"

I have become the official ironing guy in our home. You can call me Iron Man.

Jesus said, "For even I, the Son of Man, came here not to be served but to serve others, and to give My life as a ransom for many" (Matt. 20:28, author's paraphrase).

All of us start out in life being "me-focused." We live in our own "YOUniverse." But relationships require a servant's attitude in order to flourish. Jesus said, "Whoever wants to become great among you must be your servant" (Matt. 20:26, *NIV*).

When we read the apostle Paul's instructions about marriage in Ephesians 5, he begins his direction with, "Submit to one another out of reverence for Christ" (v. 21, *NIV*). Only then does he talk about the roles of the husband and the wife. Marriage requires a mutual yielding and an intention to serve the other person.

When we are single, we tend to live thinking life is all about us. It's not. It's not all about what we feel, about expressing ourselves or fulfilling our dreams. What's going to make a relationship flourish is not making your dreams come true as much as it is getting really good at serving each other.

When you are looking at a life-partner candidate, ask yourself this important question: Does he serve others in any capacity?

Does he help out with errands or household tasks when the need is there?

Does he visit the sick?

Is he willing to do family chores?

Does he volunteer at church?

Is he willing to be a mentor to disadvantaged youth?

Is he involved in causes in the local community?

Is he "others-minded"?

All of us have room to grow in this area. To evaluate a person you are dating, I suggest you develop your own private "servant scale." On a scale of 1 to 10, is he a 2 or a 6? Be honest. Pay attention. After some time has gone by, reevaluate; has his rating gone up or down? If his "serve-itude" has increased, great! But if he holds steady at a 2 or 3, look deep into his eyes and see if you don't glimpse red flags waving in the distance. If he can't serve others, he can't serve you—and marriage always boils down to serving one another. When people cannot make that turn, the relationship breaks down.

Bob Dylan wrote a song called "Gotta Serve Somebody." It may be your spouse. It may be yourself. It may be your own appetites. It may be others. It may be the Lord. You get to choose, but you're gonna have to serve somebody.

If you want to learn more about "relationship red flags" from Holly and me, you can see some short videos and other resources at www.godchicks.com.

Just for the Men!

She thinks she wants the fairy tale.

She is tempted by the fairy tale, but who wants to kiss a frog, really? And what woman in her right mind wants to fall into a coma and be kissed awake by some guy who goes around kissing women in comas? Fairy tales are odd.

Women believe in our potential and are wired to see it. God gave them an innate ability to see the best in someone; they can often spot talents, gifts and abilities in their youngest form, and feel a desire to draw them out. This dynamic can set a woman up to be a mother to a man, not a wife, because she wants to help him grow into his potential.

But we must love our GodChick as God intended.

We need to love the woman in our world well, and that means protecting her. The minute we see the potential for her values or her personal value to be compromised, we must sound the alarm.

We have to be smarter about love.

Be love smart; be smarter about the issues of the heart.

King Solomon told us, "Guard your heart above all else because it determines the course of your life" (Prov. 4:23, *NIV*). Who or what we allow into our heart can shape the rest of our life. Make sure you are the kind of man who shapes her life for the better.

Don't get too close too soon. And if you are in a relationship with a woman who will never be your wife, be honest and cut her loose. It's not fair to lead her on.

Be a man who is dedicated to personal growth.

Choose to be in a relationship with someone who is compatible with you.

Know what your values are. Stand strong in them and choose a woman who can partner with you in those values.

Don't be emotionally reckless. Make sober-minded decisions about your life and purpose.

Be a student of life and a servant of others.

The woman in your world will know what to expect from others because she watches you.

Notes

1. Gordon Livingston, M.D., *How to Love* (New York: De Capo Lifelong Books, 2009), p. xiii.
2. K.C. Baker, "The Kiss We Build Our Dreams On . . . New Research Shows Our First Smooch Is Our Strongest, Most Sensual Memory," *New York Daily News*, June 17, 1999. https://www.nydailynews.com/archives/lifestyle/1999/06/17/1999-06-17_the_kiss_we_build_our_dreams.html (accessed January 2010).
3. Gordon Livingston, M.D., *How to Love*, p. xxii.
4. C. E. Rollins, *Are We Compatible?* (Nashville, TN: Thomas Nelson, Inc., 1995), p. 135.

5

Irreconcilable Differences

(Holly)

United we stand. Divided we fall.
AESOP

What I do, you cannot do; but what you do, I cannot do.
The needs are great, and none of us, including me, ever do
great things. But we can all do small things, with great love,
and together we can do something wonderful.
MOTHER TERESA OF CALCUTTA

But at the beginning of creation God "made them male and female."
"For this reason a man will leave his father and mother and be united to his
wife, and the two will become one flesh." So they are no longer two, but one.
Therefore what God has joined together, let man not separate.
MARK 10:6-9, NIV

Not long ago, I saw a young woman fall over 100 feet from a construction platform onto hard ground. She was bloody and broken. Her head was turned almost 180 degrees from where it should be. And then, in just moments, I saw her get up.

A few days later, she stuck her hand into a garbage disposal where it got totally chewed up. When she pulled her hand out, the bones could be seen. Gross. But then, within minutes, the bones repaired themselves and the skin regenerated! It was so cool!

Okay. This wasn't real life. It was an episode of the TV show *Heroes.*

In this show, there are a handful of people with very special, highly evolved DNA, which makes them different. They each have very special abilities. And I must confess, there are moments when I wish I had some of their special abilities. How cool would it be to fly? Or to travel through time?

Their differences make for an interesting TV show . . . but in reality, we are more alike than different.

Through the 1990s until 2003, geneticists conducted research called the Human Genome Project. This project set out to determine the complete structure of human genetic material. There were many intriguing findings, but the most interesting to me was the conclusion that human beings, at the genetic level, are almost 99-percent identical. We are way more alike than we are different.[1]

You might look different than me. Maybe your skin is darker. Maybe your eyes are brown. Maybe you have freckles or your hair is curly. Maybe your feet are flat. Perhaps you are five feet tall or your body responds differently to penicillin. All these differences may seem significant, but they make up only 1 percent of our DNA. All of us, each one of us reading this, are almost 99-percent identical.

I think we might get further in life and in fulfilling God's plan if we focus on where we are the same.

Sometimes we are *so* adamant that our 1 percent is recognized that, instead of focusing on what we are all trying to do together— on what we can accomplish together—we let our 1 percent create division.

God put you and me on the planet at this time in history to fulfill His purpose . . . not our own. He made us how He made us so that together we would see His purpose done. We are all supposed to be working together, in harmony and unity.

One definition of unity is "acting as a single entity." Unity is *not* being the same, but all of us, with all of our differences, headed in the same direction . . . walking as one. French author Antoine de Saint-Exupery wrote, "Life has taught us that love does not consist in gazing at each other, but in looking outward together in the same direction." We cannot move forward together if we are obsessed with keeping track of all our differences.

Our unity is *so* central to the heart of God, so crucial to the planet, that Jesus prayed about it right before He went to the cross. In that prayer, we find an invitation into oneness, not only with God but also with each other.

The goal is for all of them to become one heart and mind—
Just as you, Father, are in me and I in you,
So they might be one heart and mind with us.
Then the world might believe that you, in fact, sent me.
JOHN 17:21, THE MESSAGE

Togetherness. Unity. Oneness. This idea is a *very* big deal to God—
and has been from the beginning:

And the Lord said, Behold, they are *one people* and they have
all *one language*; and this is only the beginning of what they
will do, and now *nothing they have imagined they can do will be
impossible for them* (Gen. 11:6, emphasis added).

In the story surrounding these Scriptures, the people were using
the power of unity to create something contrary to God and His
plans. So God had to divide them. But the principal of the power of
our unity is the issue here.

I am still trying to wrap my head around this promise. If you and
I become one people—not the same, but a people united, speaking
one language . . . not the same language, but a united language—then
NOTHING WILL BE IMPOSSIBLE FOR US.

Nothing. Not the AIDS crisis. Not the plight of the orphan. Not
cancer. Not crime. Not loneliness.

When we are united, everything is possible. We can feed the poor.
We can rescue the hurting. We can reach lost people. We can grow
thriving churches.

We can build strong marriages.

You and I must unite around the 99 percent, rather than letting
the 1 percent distract and divide us. Our differences are there to
make life interesting, not to separate.

Yes, you are different than your spouse—only 1-percent different on a genetic level, but it may seem like much more. These differences are supposed to bring strength, but sadly, they are often cause
for division. We are different genders, have different personalities,
have different likes and dislikes, and probably come from different
backgrounds; there are a lot of differences that can divide unless we
seek unity.

Cultivate Unity

Becoming one heart and mind will take more than emotion, more than singing about it, more than writing poems about it. It will require more than lighting the unity candle during your wedding ceremony. Did you light the unity candle as part of your ceremony?

It goes something like this:

At a certain point in the wedding ceremony, there are two lit candles, representing the distinct lives of the bride and groom before their wedding day. The bride and groom each take one candle, and together light the center candle to symbolize the union of their individual lives.

The minister might say something like this: "As this new flame burns undivided, so shall your lives now be one. From now on, your thoughts will always be for each other rather than for your individual selves."

In most ceremonies, the bride and groom then extinguish the two flames symbolizing their previous lives because they are now forever united together in love.

I like this part of the wedding ceremony. But I know, after 25 years of marriage, that unity did not come because we lit a candle.

In reality, it is more like this: We each have a box of broken pieces and parts, representing our personalities, quirks and backgrounds. We have the chance to combine our boxes and build something amazing. Maybe we should add the box of pieces to the wedding ceremony for the sake of accuracy, but here's the kicker: Building unity takes a long time.

Establishing unity requires cultivation. The apostle Paul put it like this: "I have a serious concern to bring up with you, my friends, using the authority of Jesus, our Master. I'll put it as urgently as I can: You must get along with each other. You must learn to be considerate of one another, *cultivating* a life in common" (1 Cor. 1:10, *THE MESSAGE*, emphasis added).

Let's look at some definitions of the word "cultivate."

1. To bestow attention, care, and labor upon, with a view to valuable returns.
2. To direct special attention to; to devote time and thought to; *to foster; to cherish.*
3. To improve by labor, care.[2]

Do I *cherish* unity? That definition stands out to me. Do we cherish unity or do we cherish our own way? Do we want to be right or do we want to be married? Adopting a spirit of unity in our marriage means preferring our partner over ourselves, devoting special attention, providing thoughtful care and fostering an environment where our spouse and our relationship can flourish.

I am not talking about being a doormat or suffering through abuse. I am talking about the day-in-day-out laying down of our lives and our egos. Jesus says it best: "Greater love has no one than this: that he lay down his life for his friends" (John 15:13). Although Jesus did lay down His life for us, and there could very well come a time when you and I might need to give up our life for someone, I actually think that verse has broader implications. I think Jesus asks us to give up our way, our ego and what is convenient.

Do you know what?

Sometimes I think taking a bullet for Philip might be easier than laying down my wants. But cherishing unity means laboring together to build a life, a legacy, a living example of Christ's love for His church on the earth.

Cultivate unity.

"Cultivation" sounds like a gardening word. I am not a gardener, but when my children were young I was looking for projects to do with them. We had a large patch of dirt in our back yard, so I thought planting carrots together would be a great idea. It was their favorite vegetable, so I figured they would get into this project too. I bought the seeds and we went out to plant them. Each of us took our finger and made little rows in the dirt. We put the seeds in them, covered them up and watered the whole area. Eventually green leaves started to come through the dirt. Yea!

We were getting excited just thinking about the beautiful, big carrots growing hidden in the dirt. When the green leaves got long enough, we went out to pull out the carrots. We took a big basket because we just knew that we'd fill the whole thing up. Well, we pulled out carrots all right—but they were severely stunted. They were about an inch long and two inches wide. We were shocked! What happened to our carrots?!

Because I had not cultivated the ground, the carrots could not grow. The dirt was too hard. Bummer. (So much for carrots in the salad that night!)

Cultivation requires work and it requires tools . . . tools like wisdom and patience. And a willingness to get a little dirty. There is no cultivation of anything without a willingness to get a little messy. My carrots did not grow because I didn't have the right tools and I was not willing to get dirty, to get in the dirt and till the ground. My carrot project was doomed from the beginning!

The ultimate purpose of cultivating the ground is to produce fruit, not just to play in the dirt. The focus is on the fruit. Can we focus on the fruit our unity might produce instead of on the hard work that cultivating it demands?

Vive la Différence!

Recently I read a science fiction book about clones. Very cool. This young girl had been cloned and so grew up with three other girls just like her. They all had the same name, same personality, same movements and lived the same life. There were no differences to create conflict. Together, they pulled off the perfect crime: While one was committing the crime, another created the perfect alibi by putting herself where witnesses could see her at the gym. (The story has absolutely nothing to do with this book, but it was thrilling and I thought you might enjoy it. Now back to the point . . .)

Because you and your husband are not two clones, you have differences . . . and those differences will create conflict. When handled maturely, conflict is a very good thing. Conflict can deepen a relationship and sharpen us as individuals, making us stronger as a couple.

A couple's ability to deal with differences is a sign of their maturity. Children demand that others agree with them. Immature couples do the same. An immature husband calls his wife "selfish" and has a tantrum when his wife does not see things his way. An immature wife gets discouraged when things aren't perfect and withdraws in resignation, mumbling that "we'll just never see eye to eye." Such spouses cannot live with the tension that the other person won't change his or her mind, and they easily become prey to intruders who agree with them. He might begin to think, *The woman at my work is so much more like me.* She might begin to wonder, *Do I have more in common with that man I meet at school functions?*

In reality, "annoying" differences pop up in any new relationship. Maturity involves working through the differences in the marriage you now have. Grownups attempt to understand the other's viewpoint while holding on to their own reality. They empathetically appreciate the opinions of the other person and work toward a negotiated agreement, based on love, sacrifice, values and principles. Differences do not create intruder problems; immaturity does.[3]

Philip and I have been married for 25 years, and most of them have been great. But there have been moments when I wondered if we would make it another year. Our differences have been our biggest challenge. Honestly, we still deal with them—because Philip is still who he is and I am still who I am. We have certainly grown over the years, but we will never be each other. I will only ever be a better version of me. I will never be him.

I have talked to hundreds of couples over the years, and every single one of them, at some point in their relationship, said, "We are just too different. We have irreconcilable differences."

Well, duh! We all have differences.

Honestly, you wouldn't be attracted to someone who isn't different than you. (I think God watches us as we are dating and thinks, *This is going to be fun!*)

Marriage is a lifelong process of learning to love the differences. When I ask couples who have been married less than 15 years what they would change about their spouse, they usually have a list. But when I ask couples who have been married more than 40 years the same question, they usually say they wouldn't change a thing. What happens during those 25 years or so?

Couples who take on the challenge of understanding their differences grow to love those differences.

When we are dating, we might notice the differences but we don't see that they could ever be a challenge—because we are "in love," that brain-dead state where reality is nowhere within reach. This is the time in a relationship when you will go to every sporting event known to man just because you want to be with him. This is the time when he will take you to chick flicks and say things like, "I could hold you forever." He can do no wrong. It all feels great, this cloudy, in-love, euphoric feeling. Awesome.

Experts say it can last up to two years.

Mature love is what you do when the exciting, euphoric feelings aren't there. If we want to cultivate unity, we must move into mature love, which is much stronger because it doesn't rely on a cloudy feeling. If we don't move into maturity, then when the euphoric feeling is not there, we leave or withdraw, maybe divorce, hoping to find that feeling again.

I knew a woman who was in the middle of a divorce from Husband No. 1. She had been married to him for about a year, and they had dated about a year before that. The exciting, heart-fluttering feelings just weren't there anymore—and she wanted out. She wanted those feelings. She wasn't willing to go to a seminar, read books, talk to a counselor or get help building real love. When I met her, she was already on to the next relationship. She had found a new man, and all of those exciting feelings were there. The sad thing is that she thought that her new relationship would end up differently than the first one. It didn't. After a year or so, she just didn't have those feelings. This cycle could go on forever until she is willing to take the journey of real love.

Part of that journey is learning to accept the differences and letting them bring strength to the relationship.

So what are some of the differences we must learn to deal with?

Differences of gender. Obvious. *Vive la différence!*

There are some great books out there, written by some very smart people, that can help you cultivate an appreciation for these differences. I will just touch on a few here, but we should recognize that there are always exceptions. Your husband may not be the typical male and you may not be the typical female—but there will still be differences.

In biology class, I learned that there are two sides to our brain. You probably learned this, too. There is the left side and the right side (complicated, isn't it?). The sides are connected by a thick bundle of nerves called the corpus callosum. This bundle of nerves is wider in women, which allows more "crosstalk" between the two sides of the brain.[4]

This difference in brain structure means that there are differences between women and men on a very basic level. Some are interesting. Some might drive you nuts. ☺

Women listen equally with both ears. Men tend to turn their right one toward the person who is speaking. This fact will not save your marriage; I just found it interesting.

Females are generally better at reading emotions of people, whether live or even in photographs. Men seem to be able to rotate three-dimensional objects in their head, which is why most men are generally better at reading maps. Women usually turn the map in the direction we're going. (Perhaps all this crosstalk between the left and right sides of the brain keeps the brain from doing its job—which is focusing on the map!)

So he can read a map . . . but can he find his socks?

Women are about 70 percent better than men at remembering the locations of items found on a desktop, which is why we can usually recall the location of apparently unconnected items.[5] (This is why we can find the socks that he left by the desk.)

When my children need help finding something, they come to me—because "we need a mom kind of look." Philip opens the refrigerator and yells, "Where's the mustard?" From the other side of the house I yell back, "It's on the top shelf!" I quit getting bugged by his mustard-blindness, because it is just the brain thing.

Women tend to talk more. This is probably not a surprise. (Comedian Jimmy Durante was once heard to remark, "My wife has a slight impediment in her speech. Every now and then she stops to breathe.")

Generally men talk to communicate information.

We talk for lots of reasons; information is just one. We also talk to figure out what we really want to say. This used to drive Philip nuts. I would be talking away in my closet while getting dressed, and he would call from the bedroom, "Am I supposed to be hearing this? Because I can't."

I'd yell back, "Nope. I'm just thinking out loud."

We also talk to create a sense of intimacy. Men usually want the end result of the intimacy, so this is where they have to become great listeners. But we can help them. I have learned that if I say to Philip, "Could I talk to you for about 15 minutes?" then he knows that there is a beginning and, thank God, there will be an end. Sometimes we feel the need to share every detail of our day, and really, he just wants the highlights. That's okay. If you need to share every detail of your trip to the dentist, call a girlfriend. She will appreciate them.

We usually handle stress differently. We all feel stress—and not all stress is bad—but we probably handle it in varying ways. Men generally isolate themselves when they feel stressed. John Gray, in his book *Men*

Are from Mars; Women Are from Venus, wrote that a man goes to his "cave," someplace where he can shut off his brain. He doesn't want to talk. He doesn't really want to think. He just wants a remote control and a TV, or a ball and a court, or tennis shoes and a trail. I made the mistake in the early days of our marriage of thinking Philip was like me. When women are stressed, we want to congregate. We want to talk about it. *All* about it. We want to explore all the aspects of how stressed we are. I think I drove Philip crazy the first year, because when he was stressed he would try to isolate himself, and I would chase after him asking him questions, which is what I would want him to do for me. And he just kept looking for his cave. Eventually he did want to talk about what was stressing him, but the talking happened after he had his own processing time. Very different than me.

Women are usually more intuitive about the needs of others. If I see someone shivering, I think, "I will turn on the heater." But usually a man won't turn on the heater unless he is asked. He figures that if someone needs help, they will ask for it. I used to get so frustrated when Philip couldn't tell that I needed a hug. My sad little face wasn't enough of a clue! But I learned that if I need a hug or some time with him, I needed to ask—and he is happy to do it, because he loves me, wants to do the right thing and wants a "win." Men are not mind readers. They will not pick up on the clues, no matter how obvious. Just ask.

I have read so many articles and books and listened to many teachings on gender differences, and one thing I have noticed is that, in many ways, Philip is not the typical male.

He will stop for directions. More than once. I am the one who would rather figure it out.

He can't fix anything. And doesn't want to try.

He has no idea what to do with a BBQ pit.

He does not make quick decisions.

So, while there are some typically common gender differences, you and your husband might not fit the box.

Isn't marriage exciting?

Background Colors

Philip and I come from very different family backgrounds. You and your partner might, too. A lot of the initial conflict in a marriage exists as we try to bring our different backgrounds together. Maybe your husband's mother was a stay-at-home mom who cooked dinner every night, and you are a teacher or a doctor. The dinner hour might have to work differently than he is used to. Maybe your dad was controlling or abusive, or isolated himself from the rest of your family. That will affect your expectations as you try to build your marriage. We can't pretend that our assumptions are not colored by our background or that we don't bring any baggage from our childhoods into our marriage.

Maybe you were raised in a home where there was not much physical affection. I am sorry about that, because physical affection is a good thing. I was raised in a home where I was hugged and kissed every day. I was told regularly that I was loved and was supported in all of my endeavors. I saw affection between my parents—lots of hugging and kissing went on! Philip, on the other hand, was raised in a home without much affection. His parents divorced when he was an adolescent, and before the divorce there was quite a bit of anger and fighting.

When Philip and I were engaged, my parents came to California to visit me. Philip and I went to the airport to pick them up—this was back in the day when we could go to the gate to meet people! I saw my parents walking down the jetway, and as soon as my dad was through, I ran, jumped in his arms, hugging him. He began to twirl me around. As I was being hugged and twirled, I caught a glimpse of Philip's face: His mouth was open and his chin had hit his chest. He was stunned at this display of affection between a father and daughter.

As Philip and I began to build our marriage, we had to figure out how to navigate our different backgrounds. He liked the affection thing and wanted it to be in our family, so now he does a lot of hugging and kissing! But I had to be patient while he got comfortable with it.

Yes, Philip and I had quite a few background differences. He was raised in the United States; I was raised all over the world. He had four siblings; I had one.

Maybe you were raised with money, while he was raised cutting coupons. You will have to have some necessary conversations to navigate how you want to build your family.

Maybe you were raised in another country speaking a different language, while he was raised on good ole American apple pie. One of the women in my world was raised in a mud hut in Kenya. She came to the U.S. and received her education here, and ultimately married an American man who went to an Ivy League university. In order to marry her, I think he had to pay a bride price of 13 camels or something to her father.

They have had a few background differences to work through!

The Language(s) of Love

Another difference we might need to navigate is how we feel loved. Gary Chapman's bestselling book *The Five Love Languages* is a great help in this area.[6] In a nutshell, he says that while we all want and need to feel loved, how we receive love may be different from our spouse. We each have a language of love.

Because I plan on being married to Philip for lots of years, I want to be great at speaking his love language. Learning that language is my responsibility. If I speak the language I want instead of the language that he understands, not much effective communication will happen.

Si yo empese a escribir en Espanol, solamente las personas que hablan Espanol me pueden entender. Si yo sigue escribiendo en Espanol, las personas que no intienden Espanol se van a poner frustrado, porque quieren entender, pero no se pueden.

If I kept writing the rest of this chapter in Spanish or Wingdings, most of you wouldn't read it—not because you don't like me, but because you don't speak Spanish or Wingdings. Only people who understand Spanish or Wingdings could understand what I am writing. Everyone else would want to understand . . . but just couldn't.

Gary Chapman describes five love languages. While we all like each of these expressions of love, there is only one that is our "native" language. The first one is *words of affirmation*. Verbal compliments. Words of appreciation. Encouraging words. Kind words. This is Philip's primary love language, so I better get great at speaking words of affirmation.

"You look great today."

"That was an awesome message you gave on Sunday."

Honestly, when I am irritated, nice words are the first thing to go. I want to say words to him . . . only, they are not nice.

Another love language is *quality time*. You feel loved when you get time with your spouse. Uninterrupted, focused time. Alone time. Time when you are listened to. I have a friend whose primary love language is quality time, but it is not her husband's. He is certainly happy to see her, but he doesn't need lots of time with her to feel loved. He asked me how he could get better at speaking her language. What we realized was that if she gets one hour a day with him, she feels totally loved. So that's what he does.

Maybe your primary love language is *gifts*. Now, we all like presents, but you may feel loved when your husband brings you flowers or writes you a note or gives you something in a Tiffany's blue box!

For some, their primary love language might be what Gary Chapman calls *acts of service*. This person feels loved when someone does something for her: laundry, dishes, getting bugs off the windshield, cleaning up dog poop . . . whatever. And this person might feel unloved if she comes home and the counters are filthy, dishes are piled up and her car is returned with the gas gauge on empty.

The last love language is *physical touch*. This is my primary language, so Philip has had to get great at it. Remember, he did not come from a family that spoke this language, so he had to learn it. It *is* possible to learn a language you did not grow up speaking. And he has. Obviously, sexual intercourse is part of physical touch, but it is more. Holding hands. Patting. Putting his arm around me. Kissing. Hugging.

We must learn to speak the language of our spouse's heart. The movie *Love Actually* follows a few different people on their quests for love. There are some fairly explicit scenes so I can't really recommend the movie, but I do want to highlight one particular couple. The woman could speak only Portuguese, and the man could speak only

English. He was a writer and she was hired to clean his house. Because they couldn't understand each other's words, they had to learn to communicate by other means. By the end of the movie, they had fallen in love with each other—and both of them took classes so that they could speak the other's language.

Speaking each other's language demonstrates honor and value. Love is about giving, so you and I need to be great at giving. What does your spouse need? It is not all about what you need. I have also found that as I start giving, I usually get everything I need. Sometimes we stop giving or trying because we are irritated. We withdraw. We hold back. Not good. Grown-up love involves going beyond. Learn to speak his language.

Good Personalities

Early in our marriage, personality differences were the biggest challenge for Philip and me.

Organizations all over the country administer personality profiles to their employees so that they can place people in jobs where they will flourish and the employees will function better together. There have been many different profiles developed in recent years, but Hippocrates (460-370 B.C.) was the first to begin the discussion. It continues today with the DiSC Assessment, the Keirsey Temperament Sorter, the Myers-Briggs Type Indicator, and many others. I find these helpful—not to put someone in a box, but to better communicate and understand the people in my world.

We are usually a blend of a few temperaments. There is no right or wrong personality. No personality is better than another, and each has strengths and weaknesses.

Our personality is God-given. He created us to fulfill a purpose on the earth, and it will require our personality. It's interesting to me that two people who marry each other usually have very different personality styles. We are usually attracted to someone who is different than we are. This can be a good thing! We have strengths where they have weaknesses, and vice versa.

Sounds good, doesn't it?

My weaknesses are compensated by his strengths, so that together we are stronger.

Yep, definitely sounds good.

Only, his weaknesses can be very annoying. I am sure that mine never are.

As far as personality goes, I am not sure Philip and I could be any more different.

I am the fast-talking, energetic, out-of-the-box, never-a-dull-moment kind of girl. I laugh a lot, see the glass half-full, look for opportunities to have fun, and like being with people. I am goal-driven and make decisions quickly. I like people to like me, and am always a bit surprised when someone doesn't. I am a loyal friend. I make new ones easily and have kept some for more than 25 years.

That's the good stuff.

On the flip side, I get impatient if someone isn't moving fast enough. I often need the approval of others too much. I might finish your sentences for you. I can talk too much. I can be loud and just a bit pushy.

Annoying, aren't I?

Philip is generally mild-mannered. He is compassionate. He likes organization. He gets where he is going on time. He is very funny. He is creative. He is loyal. He is a great thinker and a perpetual learner. He is great at ironing (wrinkles bother his need for order). He notices the details. He is a great planner. He thinks before he speaks. He listens.

There is probably lots more good stuff.

On the flip side, he often notices what is wrong before he notices what is right. He can be critical. He likes things to go a certain way and when they don't, it affects him. He can be slow to make decisions.

And all of those can annoy me.

One day, during the first year of our marriage, Philip told me that we should wash my car. Sounded like fun to me! He brought out the bucket filled with sudsy water, a few sponges to do the washing and a hose. The hose had a nozzle on the end that allowed water to be sprayed. I took one look at that hose, then grabbed it and sprayed Philip. It just seemed like the fun, spontaneous thing to do in that moment. I was fully prepared for him to get into the fun by throwing water at me, too.

He did not quite see it that way. In fact, he was not happy.

What was he there to do? To wash the car.

I was there to play. Washing the car was secondary.

Anyone see a problem here?

We worked through that situation and many others. We have learned to value each other. And (this is important) to laugh. Not at each other—at some of the ways we are different.

Whether you have married someone who is very similar to you with a lot of the same strengths and weaknesses (scary thought) or someone quite different, it takes a bit of effort to go from hating your differences to understanding them, and eventually to valuing them.

Don't expect your spouse to be like you. I don't expect Philip to be Mr. Social. I know that after he has been at a function for a few hours, he's ready for some quiet time. I don't resent that about him; I just accept it. At the same time, he has no problem with my desire to be with people. He is not threatened by my friendships. Actually, he says that my focus on people has helped him include more people in our life.

We all have "irreconcilable differences."

All of us.

They are not so evident when we are in that brain-dead, euphoric, cloudy state when we are dating—or if they are obvious, we don't mind them. When Philip and I were dating, I loved the fact that his car was always clean and that he showed up on time. Eventually, however, I called his punctuality and need for order "picky."

He loved my spontaneity and my carefree ability to make everything fun. Eventually, he saw them as careless and irresponsible.

Same personality traits . . . we just looked at them differently.

The journey we have made and continue to make is to look for the strengths and forgive the weaknesses.

Recently, Philip and I both spoke at a church. A few days later, the pastor was making some comments about both of us and laughingly said, "Wow, you are both so different in your energy levels and styles. I am impressed that you have stayed married!"

Not only have we stayed married, but we also actually like each other.

And if we can do it, so can you!

There are plenty of differences that can divide, but I encourage you to see them as bringing strength to the whole.

Yes, there are differences, but perhaps we need to focus on where we are similar. If we continue to emphasize where we are different, we can get frustrated, or even think of the other person as "wrong." So how about focusing on where you are the same?

Here's our list:

- We both love God.
- We both love each other.
- We are both committed to our marriage.
- We both love our children.
- We both love building the Church.
- We both love our friends.
- We both love playing with other people's babies.
- We both love to travel.
- We both love the beach.
- We both love to read.
- We both love to laugh.
- We both love sitting in coffee shops and people-watching.
- We both like swimming in the ocean when it is warm.
- We both like getting massages.
- We both like to play in New York City.
- We both like living in Los Angeles.
- We both like going to conferences to learn.
- We both like to teach.
- We both like movies.
- We both like dogs.
- We both like Indian food.
- We both like Thai food.
- We both take a *lot* of vitamins.
- We both work out.
- We both will love our grandchildren.
- We both pray for our children and their future spouses.
- We both are committed to our friends.
- We both want to make a contribution to our city and world.
- We both are committed to helping the orphan.
- We both hate injustice against children.
- We both are determined to see the next generation fulfill their purpose.
- Ninety-nine percent of our DNA is the same.

We can get frustrated at the differences or we can focus on what unites us.

Make your own list.

_____

_____

_____

_____

_____

_____

_____

_____

_____

_____

_____

_____

_____

_____

_____

_____

If we are united, nothing is impossible.

The apostle Paul said it best:

I want you to think about how all this makes you more significant, not less. A body isn't just a single part blown up into something huge. It's all the different-but-similar parts arranged and functioning together. If Foot said, "I'm not elegant like Hand, embellished with rings; I guess I don't belong to this body," would that make it so? If Ear said, "I'm not beautiful like Eye, limpid and expressive; I don't deserve a place on the head," would you want to remove it from the body? If the body was all eye, how could it hear? If all ear, how could it smell? As it is, we see that God has carefully placed each part of the body right where he wanted it.

But I also want you to think about how this keeps your significance from getting blown up into self-importance. *For no matter how significant you are, it is only because of what you are a part of.* An enormous eye or a gigantic hand wouldn't be a body, but a monster. What we have is one body with many parts, each its proper size and in its proper place. No part is important on its own. Can you imagine Eye telling Hand, "Get lost; I don't need you"? Or, Head telling Foot, "You're fired; your job has been phased out"? As a matter of fact, in practice it works the other way—the "lower" the part, the more basic, and therefore necessary. You can live without an eye, for instance, but not without a stomach. When it's a part of your own body you are concerned with, it makes no difference whether the part is visible or clothed, higher or lower. You give it dignity and honor just as it is, without comparisons. If anything, you have more concern for the lower parts than the higher. If you had to choose, wouldn't you prefer good digestion to full-bodied hair?

The way God designed our bodies is a model for understanding our lives together as a church: *every part dependent on every other part,* the parts we mention and the parts we don't, the parts we see and the parts we don't. If one part hurts, every other part is involved in the hurt, and in the healing. *If one part flourishes, every other part enters into the exuberance* (1 Cor. 12:14-26, *THE MESSAGE,* emphasis added).

For more help learning to navigate the differences, and for a few laughs, check out a short video from Philip and me at www.godchicks.com.

Just for the Men!

Differences can divide us unless we cultivate unity.

You married your wife because you wanted to build a life with her. Hopefully, you are reading this because you still do! The differences between you and your wife were noticeable when you were dating, but perhaps they have become an irritation as time has gone by.

Jesus asks us to live as one in spite of our differences. This is not always easy to do, but it is well worth the work.

Your wife is different than you. She probably talks more. She feels everything. The differences in your backgrounds might cause misunderstandings. Her personality is different than yours. She is either the outgoing one or the calm, peaceful one. (Right now you might be seeing her as loud and pushy or too quiet and critical.)

So . . . lots of differences.

But what if your differences are actually meant to make you stronger? Thank goodness she can remember where the keys are and seems to always know when something is going on with your teenagers. Or maybe that's you. And thank goodness you can plan things out, get places on time and help make decisions. Or maybe that's her. Your differences are supposed to make the two of you stronger, so it is well worth it to learn how to navigate them. She is a gift to you. Her strengths are needed. Together, you can learn and grow and change into your best selves as your differences sharpen and strengthen you as individuals and as a couple.

Try this: Forget your differences and focus on your similarities.

Instead of focusing on the differences that seem irreconcilable (and we all have them), write down a list of your similarities. For a while, focus on those. As you focus on your commonalities, you will remember why you chose her in the first place.

And you will discover that you are much more similar than you are different.

Notes

1. "Human Genome Project," Microsoft Encarta Online Encyclopedia, 2009. http://encarta. msn.com ©1997-2009 Microsoft Corporation.
2. *Webster's Revised Unabridged Dictionary* (MICRA, Inc., 1996), s.v. "cultivate."
3. Dr. Henry Cloud and Dr. John Townsend, *Boundaries in Marriage* (Grand Rapids, MI: Zondervan, 2002), p. 164.
4. Renato Me. Sabbatini, PhD., "Are There Differences Between the Brains of Males and Females," Brain and Mind. http://www.cerebromente.org.br/n11/mente/eisntein/cerebro-homens.html (accessed January 2010).
5. Christine Gorman and J. Madeleine Nash, "Sizing Up the Sexes," *Time Magazine*, January 20, 1992. http://www.time.com/time/magazine/article/0,9171,974689,00.html (accessed December 2009).
6. Gary Chapman, *The Five Love Languages: How to Express Heartfelt Commitment to Your Mate* (Chicago, IL: Northfield Publishing, 1995).

6

You Had Me at Hello

(Philip)

Love isn't blind, it just only sees what matters.
ANONYMOUS

Love each other with genuine affection, and take delight in honoring each other.
ROMANS 12:10, *NLT*

The dreams of little girls are fragile. The dreams of women are crucial. And dreams make life inspiring.

Rachel dreams about a handsome man who will sweep her away.

Karla dreams of being a princess.

April has hopes of a family one day—times of laughter, love and support.

Donna wants to start and manage a successful business.

Sheila dreams of a boyfriend who will love her.

Simone wants to be in full-time ministry.

Dreams are magnetic and powerful. A woman's dreams are vital to her heart.

Every woman dreams of being loved, truly loved, by a man who adores her—a man who cares more about her than his career. (Is that possible?) She may desire a man who is smarter, stronger and more handsome than any other. Women who love God want a man who has faith and is passionate about life.

But mostly girls dream about a man who will love, honor and be there for her.

Women want someone they can trust at the deepest level!

In the movie *Jerry Maguire*, Tom Cruise plays the part of a sports agent. Jerry is struggling in his career to establish his own agency. In his attempt to make it, he is trying to sign the NFL receiver he represents to a big contract. This will establish him as a legitimate agent, validating his agency and securing his career as an independent agent.

His wife, Dorothy, helps to make it all happen, but Jerry focuses on his goal and loses sight of his relationship with her. He finally lands the contract, but he realizes that without the love of his life to share this moment, his victory means nothing.

Jerry goes to find Dorothy in order to repair the damage he has done by his neglect. He finds her in the living room, in a support-group meeting full of frustrated women who don't trust men so much anymore. He stands in front of all these women to declare his love for his wife. He attempts to describe how much he values her, how much he honors her and how meaningless his life is without her.

As he stumbles through his apologies, stutters through a description of his revelation, he begins expressing his love for her . . . right there in front of God and everybody.

I remember cringing in the theater during this scene. I get embarrassed for people when they are embarrassing themselves. I was worried. *Where is this going? Is he going to make this worse? Is she going to tell him to get out?*

But my anxiety was unnecessary, because he does a really great job!

Jerry goes on and on, saying all the honoring and loving things that should have been said long ago. But then Dorothy interrupts—she has heard enough!

"Shut up . . . just shut up. You had me at 'hello.' "

You had me at "hello"? How is that possible?

When someone tries to sincerely convey how much he loves you, when he is expressing from the heart the honor he feels for you, it can be felt beyond the words he speaks. Honoring is powerful. That kind of love is healing. It's engaging. That's it! That's the kind of love that every woman desires, the kind of loving honor that Dorothy had been waiting for. Every woman wants a man who will declare his love publicly before God, humanity and even a room full of the disillusioned. The heart of every woman in that living-room support group is touched, because the lack of loving honor is what brought each of them to that meeting in the first place.

Honor in the heart empowers the words coming out of the mouth. Jerry stands there, doing his best to honor Dorothy by expressing the depth of his love for her. And it's his willingness to do that—to honor her even in an embarrassing situation, putting his pride at risk—that touches her heart. That's why he has her at "hello."

The Walking Wounded

"Ladies and Gentlemen, we have a winner!"

That is what it feels like to be honored. Expressing genuine honor to someone is one of the most powerful components of a great relationship. To honor those you love is to declare their value to you, to demonstrate your appreciation of them, and to express their importance to you in a way that makes it apparent to others.

Women need to be honored. In fact, everyone needs to be honored. We are challenged in the Scripture to "give honor to whom honor is due" (Rom. 13:7). Honor is the way good people treat each other.

It is healthy for you to expect honor in relationships and in life. While you cannot demand honor from anyone, you can request it. It is important that you give honor to others as well; give and it shall be given to you.

My intention in this book is to honor you. What I want to convey to you is that *I believe in you.* I also want to present some ideas that could help you have a great relationship with the man in your life.

The world needs you to shine. We need you to flourish. We need your compassion, your heart and your contribution. Your family needs you to flourish. Your friends need you to overcome the battles you face. Your church needs your example of strength and determination. Our world needs your grace. Without what you bring to our world, life will be less than what is intended—for all of us.

God has a plan for women. You are important to God's plan.

You are important to men. You have an irreplaceable role.

Women are lovers and they are leaders. They are encouragers and they are friends. Women can turn the ordinary into the amazing. What a woman can do and who she is can bring out God's best in any situation.

If you need a great environment, include a godly woman. If you need a great team, recruit a woman with heart. If you want a great life, invite a woman whose light is shining.

But there are many amazing women whose gifts are hidden from the rest of us, hidden because of wounds of the heart.

Are you aching inside?

Have you forgotten about the magic inside you?

Are you struggling to survive?

Can you remember the inspiration you feel when you are loved?

Women need to be loved and admired by the men who are important to them; they need honor in order to flourish—but too few have that experience. Some are ignored, some are disregarded and many have their value overlooked. In the absence of admiration, a woman's uniqueness is too often hidden.

Some women suffer abuse. When this happens, not only is God's gifting not allowed to blossom, but also the light is put out. What God intended to be a light burning bright is reduced to a smoldering wick, a spiraling breath of smoke where a flame was intended.

Usually when you talk to a woman during her first two years of marriage, there are smiles, funny stories and a gleam in her eye. But on this day, sitting in my office, there was none of that. Sandy sat in an awkward silence, trying to work up the strength to describe her marriage while keeping her composure. Her moist eyes revealed pain. It seemed hard for her to breathe.

Silence often speaks louder than words.

"Where do I start? We were so in love. I don't know what happened. He seems like another man. Everything was great in the beginning, but we have just grown apart so quickly. I feel like I'm suffocating. I guess I married the wrong person. I wish I knew how to go back to what we had."

This is a familiar story. It is repeated in various forms; the names change, but the situations are recognizable.

"I love him," she continued. "But I don't know how much longer I can do this. I feel like we are just roommates who can't agree on much. He never touches me, he doesn't hold me . . . unless he wants sex. And that is not that often. I've lost respect for him and I don't trust him anymore. What can we do?"

Do you know someone in that situation? Have you been there? Perhaps we can define a road that leads to life in our relationships. Let's take a look. Maybe we can discover a path that leads us back to the love that brought us together.

The Five Qualities of a Thriving Relationship

What does it take to have a great relationship? In this day and age, is it even possible anymore? I want to offer some suggestions that I believe can help create a great relationship.

The ultimate human relationship is marriage. Holly and I have been married for 25 years. We have had many struggles and challenges, but we have a great relationship today. I have also coached others on their marriages. I've seen people turn their lifeless or disappointing marriages around. What looked like relationships headed for a train wreck became fulfilling and wonderful partnerships. I have learned some things in the last 25 years that I know make a marriage great.

If you truly desire to have a great marriage, let me assure you that it *is* possible. If you are single and still looking for "the one," please take the next few pages very seriously. If you are married and want to rekindle your passion into a lasting love, the following are some practical steps you can take to lead the way. If you want to enjoy a relationship based on the love you've always dreamed about, please consider these five qualities of a thriving relationship. If your relationship lacks one or more of these qualities, don't worry—we'll also explore how to develop each of these components in your relationship.

The first quality of a thriving relationship is:

Honor

If you are single and evaluating whether someone will make a good mate, start here. Does he show honor to others? Is it difficult for him to show respect for others? Does he express honor to you? Does he honor your desires, your goals and your boundaries? Or does he often disregard what is important to you? Does he try to talk you out of the standards that establish your values? Does he push you to change your dreams to accommodate his desires?

If you are married and wondering what's missing in your marriage, it may be honor. If you want to breathe some life back into a stalled relationship, add a dash of genuine honor to your marital recipe. Demonstrate how important your spouse is to you by honoring him—his strengths, his goals and his feelings.

Recognize his fears, the circumstances and situations that make him insecure, and accept him instead of criticizing. Allow him to express boundaries and leave some room for him to grow and change. Accept his likes and dislikes because you accept and admire him.

A great way to express honor is to communicate admiration. Verbalize your acceptance; express how and why you value him, and demonstrate your respect for something within him: his vision, his dreams, his incredible work ethic, the way he loves your children. When you do, there's a good chance that you'll bring new life to the relationship.

What famous person would you like to meet? Who is impressive to you?

I once got to meet Michael Jordan in person. You have to realize that MJ was a hero to me. I loved watching him play basketball. I enjoyed hearing about his story off and on the court. In my opinion, he was a once-in-a-lifetime basketball player. He was bigger than the team; he was bigger than the sport. Followers of the game still compare the best players of today to MJ. I think they always will.

Jordan was filming the movie *Space Jam* and had a temporary gym erected in a large tent on the backlot in Burbank. Some friends of mine had access to the tent and invited me along. There was a pick-up game of basketball going on with some local college and NBA players. Between games, I was introduced to Jordan; we shook hands and exchanged a casual greeting.

Are you kidding me? I just met Michael Jordan! I tried to look very cool on the outside, but on the inside I was pumped! I told everyone about that moment. It was such an honor to meet my hero. I admired him.

That was several years ago, and he doesn't call me anymore. Actually, he never called me. I never see him. Basically, I have no relationship with him. But meeting him made me realize that I could easily express more honor for MJ than I sometimes expressed for my own wife. I recognized that I needed to put some of that same enthusiastic honor into my relationship with my wife.

Who do you admire? Who would you most like to meet? Maybe you would name a celebrity like Denzel Washington, Will Smith, Taylor Swift or Julia Roberts. Would you like to meet a famous businessperson, such as MicroSoft founder Bill Gates, Meg Whitman, the former President of eBay, or Howard Schultz, founder of Starbucks? Maybe you'd like to meet a famous politician—the president of the United States, a former president or a famous senator. Maybe you might pick a well-known sports personality like A-Rod, LeBron James or Venus Williams.

Who is that someone who could make you gush with admiring words? It seems like a natural response to react that way to someone famous, but it's actually much more important that we honor those we love, the one we're building a life with.

Early in our marriage, Holly would come to me and express feelings of hurt or frustration, and I'd just get mad. She would say, "I feel like you just don't care about me."

I am pretty sure there's only one thing you are not supposed to say in that situation. Naturally, that's exactly what I said: "What? That's crazy! You shouldn't feel like that!"

Did that help the situation? No. Did it bring us closer? No. Think Vesuvius or Mt. Saint Helens, and you have an idea where that conversation went. Note to self: *If you want to push your wife toward the possibility of going postal, disregard her feelings.*

Then I tried just saying nothing. Still she would get heated.

"What?" I'd say defensively. "I didn't saying anything."

To which she would reply, "Yeah . . . but it's the way you aren't saying it."

I do love my wife and I do care about what she feels. I don't always understand what she feels—but that is *not* a good reason to withhold honor from her. Our whole rapport changed when I learned to respond to a comment like "I feel like I'm a bother to you." I learned to respond to her concerns with genuine concern, to sincerely communicate that I care: "I'm so sorry you feel that way. That must feel horrible. I'm sorry if I've done anything to make you feel like that. I never want anything I do to cause you to feel that way. What do you think I can do, even if we don't agree right now, that would make you feel loved and appreciated?"

Wow . . . completely different results!

I suggest that you put some effort into honoring the person who looks to you for love and respect. Honor him with some of the same passion you would show to a celebrity with whom you will probably never have a relationship. Don't wait for your spouse to take the lead—set the example by expressing your admiration. Without a daily injection of honor, every relationship begins to die just a little every day.

The second quality of a thriving relationship is:

Communication

Communication is another golden key to a great relationship. Good communication is about knowing what to say, how to say it and when to say it. No easy task. It takes work.

Most men communicate differently than women.

Most men need to learn to communicate better. But let me say this: No matter how good at communicating a man becomes, he will likely never communicate like a woman.

I think many a woman secretly thinks that if her husband improves in his communication ability, he will communicate more like her girlfriends. Not going to happen! I'll say more about these differences later in this chapter.

Are you at a standstill in your relationship? What are you communicating? What is the thing your spouse thinks you are conveying that weakens your relationship?

Are you considering a relationship with someone who is not a very good communicator? That is a dangerous decision. The person you allow to get involved with your heart needs to *see the importance of communication, have the desire to communicate* and *be willing to improve in that area.*

There are no other good options.

A person who is not willing to communicate or learn how to communicate is basically giving up the quality of the relationship to chance.

Years ago, I had a friend who became discouraged about our friendship. He thought I did not care about him as a person, and in fact he said something like, "I don't think you care much about me."

I asked him if he remembered the times I had invited him places, or the times I had asked him how he was doing or how he was feeling.

He said that he didn't think I had meant it.

"Well, help me understand," I said. "I invited you to meet me for coffee or go to a movie several times. Why didn't you let me know some of your concerns or feelings in those moments?"

"I didn't think you were interested," he said.

This shows a major communication breakdown. If you don't say something, how can you expect a situation to change? If we don't convey our feelings or fears, how can we hold a person accountable to our expectations?

Sometimes we think we are communicating one thing, but we are not.

We communicate in words and tone. We communicate with our attitudes and our body posture. Often we think we are saying one thing, but in reality we are communicating something else. We say one thing with our words and another with our actions. I think we just don't pay attention.

Even in what we consider love songs, the message is not communicated clearly. Many of us have heard Whitney Houston sing the song, "I Will Always Love You," from the movie *The Bodyguard*.

It's a really beautiful melody as it repeats the line "And I will always love you . . ." It sounds like such a romantic song. But if you listen to the rest of what she's saying, you realize, *This is not a love song.*

If I should stay, I'll only be in your way, so I'll go, but I know
I'll think of you every step of the way. . . .
Bittersweet memories, that is all I am taking with me, so goodbye,
please don't cry, we both know I'm not what you need.
And I . . . will always love you . . .[1]

Is this a beautiful love song? No! This is a "goodbye" song. If the one you love plays this song for you, you're in trouble.

"Wait, did I just get dropped?" Yes, like a hot potato! You are being dumped!!!

This song sounds as if it's communicating one thing, but in fact it is saying something very different.

Work on communicating clearly and effectively.

There are a few essentials that must be sought after and conveyed by both people in the relationship, if intimacy is to result: *interests, expectations, appreciation, encouragement* and *commitment* all need to be communicated clearly and passionately.

Sit down and talk. Listen first. Really listen. Then tell your story. *Communicate your interests.* Share what fascinates you. Talk about what you love so much that you want to do it for the rest of your life. What makes you feel alive? What makes you smile, from the heart?

What bores you? What do you hate so much that you will probably never change your opinion? What things have you disliked at one point in your life that you grew to enjoy later? What do you dislike that you may be able to change if it is important to someone you love?

Communicate your expectations. Expectations must be talked out. Sometimes, as we do, we discover that we have unrealistic expectations about people, marriage or life; we can save ourselves a lot of frustration by releasing those unrealistic expectations.

Sometimes we may describe an expectation we hold and find that our partner is unable or unwilling to meet that expectation. Then we have important relationship decisions to make.

What do you expect from marriage?

What do you believe a husband or wife should do or be?

What does your life need to look like in five years in order for you to be happy?

What do you expect from God, yourself and from life?

Communicate your appreciation. Expressing appreciation brings you together. It causes defenses to melt away. Tell your mate that you appreciate his efforts, his actions, his attempts and his strengths.

Tell him that you appreciate it when he says _____.

And when he doesn't say _____.

Tell him that you appreciate the gift he gave you.

Tell him the 10 things about him you are grateful for.

Tell him about the sacrifices he has made, and how much it means to you.

Tell him the qualities of character you see, admire and appreciate in him.

Post a Twitter or Facebook update about how awesome he is, and let the whole world know!

Most women like to be with a man who makes her feel safe and secure; most men tend to love a woman because of how he feels about himself when he is with her. It is a major mistake to make a man feel inadequate or uncertain, that he is always auditioning or always wrong. Communicating appreciation tells your spouse that you respect him. When your husband feels that you genuinely respect him, trust increases.

I believe that 1 bad comment can wipe out 20 positive acts of kindness. Bad comments happen, so make sure you overdose on the appreciation. Convey respect for *who he is* and *what he feels.* When you communicate appreciation for what he is doing, for his opinion and for his needs, he will trust you.

Communicate your encouragement. Encourage his attempts at being a loving father and husband.

Encourage his efforts toward improving his health.

Encourage his dependability and the provision he contributes to your family.

Encourage his spiritual hunger, his personal growth and his efforts to strengthen your relationship.

Encourage his accomplishments or achievements.

Encouragement and recognition are so important to a man. Don't forget it. Affirm what he has done and encourage what he would like to do. This will always build bridges and break down walls.

Finally, *communicate your commitment.* One of the most powerful and reassuring messages about Jesus is the biblical promise, "Never will I leave you; never will I forsake you" (Heb. 13:5, *NIV*). That is a commitment. His last words to His followers, according to Matthew, were, "I am with you always, even to the end of the age" (Matt. 28:20, *NIV*). Jesus knew how to communicate commitment.

Commitment is powerful. That's why the wedding is so important: It's the vow we make, our commitment before God, our family and friends. *Through times of sickness or health, through good times or bad, I'm committed to you.*

In the middle of a debate or argument, try communicating your commitment. Interject a reassurance about your commitment to the relationship; you'll find that commitment calms the fears of the soul.

The third quality of a thriving relationship is:

Patience

Things change. People change. Patience is the quality that allows us to gain understanding of these changes. It enables us to allow one another to get it wrong occasionally without being thrown out of the game. Two of the most valuable commodities for marriage are flexibility and adaptability, and these are perfected through patience.

Patience allows other positive qualities a chance to emerge. Kindness is a fruit of the Spirit; in other words, kindness is evidence that God is working in our heart. It takes patience to be kind, because we must be willing to delay our immediate reactions, such as "What were you thinking?!"

Patience also allows time for our perspective to be adjusted.

This perspective change was so crucial for Holly and me. We are so different in so many ways, and it would have been easier in the early days to give up. We would wonder, *How is this going to work?*

She is extremely cheerful and energetic . . . *all* the time! She makes normal people look depressed.

"Why are they so sad?" she asks.

"They are not sad; you are just . . . unusually happy. You don't realize . . . you are not normal."

Back then, I found her energy and excitement a little too much and a lot tiring. But over time, I have a new perspective. My wife's enthusiasm is contagious. She brings joy to everyone around her.

We have to change our perspective about our differences or they can bury us. We can focus on the differences as a problem or we can see them as assets that build our team. We can focus on weaknesses or strengths. Patience allows us the option to choose where we will put our focus.

The fourth quality of a thriving relationship is:

Follow-through

When you depend on someone who does what he says he will do, it is easy to trust him. And when you trust your spouse, your relationship can continue to go forward even when setbacks occur in your life.

Follow-through is important for many athletic skills, such as serving in tennis, shooting in basketball or swinging a bat in baseball. The observant coach can often help a player get back to his or her strength when he sees a breakdown in follow-through. A golfer's swing gets better results and a bowler sees his ball back in the zone when follow-through is corrected.

Follow through on the little things and follow through on the big things. Dependability is relationship glue.

Many relationships get weaker and weaker because trust has eroded.

"I just can't trust her anymore."

"He never does what he says he'll do."

Marriage can recover missing trust with an admission that you've dropped the ball or let the other down. A renewed dedication to follow-through is reassuring. Working less, spending time with the kids or being more careful with the budget are areas that all matter—but the central issue is follow-through . . . taking responsibility for your contributions, outcomes and mistakes.

"Many a man claims to have unfailing love, but a faithful man who can find?" (Prov. 20:6, *NIV*). If you are single, don't expect the undependable person you are dating to suddenly become Mr. Follow-Through two minutes after he says, "I do." If he is not dependable before the wedding, he won't magically become dependable after it.

Paul concludes his direction for marriage in Ephesians by summing it up this way: "Each one of you [husbands] also must love his wife as he loves himself, and the wife must respect her husband" (Eph. 5:33, *NIV*). We all need love and we all need respect, but there is something about the priorities of love for a woman and respect for a man. I picture the image of pedaling a bicycle to demonstrate the momentum that is possible in this dynamic. Pushing one pedal down brings the other one up. Push the other pedal down and it brings the first one up. Keep that up, and you have momentum. In marriage, the husband expresses and demonstrates love to his wife, which inspires in her respect. The wife demonstrates respect toward her husband, which empowers and motivates him to express genuine love. Keep that up, and you have momentum.

Will you be someone who will follow through? Is the man you are considering building your life with a man who will follow through?

We must continue, no matter the circumstances, to follow through on love and respect. In every marriage that stalls out, breaks up or goes through a rough patch, the husband stops loving his wife as she needs and the wife stops respecting her husband as he needs. Each one stops following through with the important ingredient he or she adds to the relationship.

To get the momentum going again, he must love her like she's the most important person in the world. She must show respect and admiration for him. That is the follow-through that is essential. I've seen this simple adjustment transform a relationship completely.

The fifth quality of a thriving relationship is:

Humility
Humility may be the most difficult character quality to develop—which is a little bit funny, since it shouldn't take much of it to realize

that we are all flawed, that we can't get it right all the time. Humility is the willingness to admit failure.

Humble people demonstrate a desire to grow. A humble husband or wife is willing to learn to recognize our spouse's needs. Humility affords us the ability to yield to the needs of the other, rather than focus wholly on our own. Humility also values the victories of others, even when victory is far removed from us. The humble are forgiving, releasing others from IOUs that steal the life out of relationships.

A humble man apologizes, forgives and prays for the ability to love his bride like Christ loves the Church. A humble woman expresses respect to her husband in a way that builds trust in his heart. She is willing to discover genuine interest in things that matter to him.

Dr. Phil, the self-help author and TV host, says, "Sometimes you make the right decision, sometimes you make the decision right." When we make a poor decision, it requires humility to admit it and correct it. Humility demands that we make the situation right by doing the right thing.

Pride kills relationships, and humility is the only antidote for pride. James encourages us to "humble yourselves before the Lord, and he will lift you up" (Jas. 4:10, *NIV*).

These are just a few qualities that build great relationships. Each one has the potential to restore joy, love and trust to the most broken of relationships.

If you want to find out more from Holly and me about qualities that build great relationships, watch some short videos at www.godchicks.com.

Just for the Men!

Women are God's secret weapon to your success and fulfillment in life, and men are vital to the health of women's souls. The world needs its women to shine, to flourish. Without what she brings to the world, we are incomplete—life is less than what was intended. Too many women and what they have to offer are hidden from us because of wounded hearts. Experiences shape us, and most women—like us—

have had some painful experiences that may cause them to hide who they really are. Honor the woman in your life. Honor is powerful. That kind of love is healing. It's engaging. And it's the kind of love every woman desires. Honoring her releases her. Honor in the heart empowers the words coming out of your mouth. Expressing honor to someone is one of the most powerful components of a great relationship. On that note . . .

Five Qualities of a Thriving Relationship

1. *Honor* is extremely important. Without a daily injection of honor, every relationship begins to die.

2. *Communication* is the golden key to a great relationship. Communicate the essentials—interests, expectations, appreciation, encouragement, commitment—clearly and effectively.

3. *Patience* allows us to choose where we will put our focus on—weaknesses or strengths.

4. *Follow-through* brings strength to a relationship because the result is trust. Why? Dependability is relationship glue.

5. *Humility* is the willingness to admit failure. Pride kills relationships, and humility is the only antidote for pride.

Note

1. Dolly Parton, "I Will Always Love You," © 1973, performed by Whitney Houston on *The Bodyguard* soundtrack, © 1992 Arista Music. Used by permission.

Sleeping with the Enemy

(Holly)

If you have only one smile in you, give it to the people you love.
Don't be surly at home, then go out in the street and start grinning
"Good morning" at total strangers.
MAYA ANGELOU

If a house is divided against itself, that house cannot stand.
MARK 3:25, *NIV*

What causes fights and quarrels among you?
Don't they come from your desires that battle within you?
JAMES 4:1, *NIV*

"This was your idea."

"No, it was yours . . . I wanted to go yesterday."

"Why are you always blaming me?"

"You never listen to me!"

"You never do what I want anyway!"

Then out she goes and slams the door.

Sounds like children, doesn't it? But this is an argument I overheard between two adults.

Most of us enter into marriage with great intentions and not many skills. So many marriages fail because people aren't willing to develop the necessary skills.

Conflicts in marriage *will* arise because we are not clones who think and act alike all the time. These conflicts can be used to strengthen or to destroy. Learning to handle conflict that rises inside and outside the marriage is crucial to the long-term health and whole-ness of the relationship.

Conflict in marriage is different than conflict on the battlefield. Your spouse is not your enemy . . . even though it feels like it some-times! Destroying your spouse, whether with hateful words, indiffer-ence or neglect, will destroy you. Because you are one.

I had a discussion one time with a woman who said that she and her husband never argued; conflict never arose in their marriage. As I spent time with them, I noticed this was basically true. I also noticed a total lack of intimacy and honesty, and a superficial level of commu-nication that would eventually lead to trouble or boredom. Allowing and resolving conflict keeps lines of communication open and gives each spouse an opportunity to air our differences.

The apostle James tells us that most of our conflict occurs be-cause of selfishness. "I want what I want, and I want it now, and you want what you want." When those desires compete, we have conflict.

Wouldn't it be easier if all of life were like the climate control in a car? The car we have has dual controls, so I can make it cooler or warmer on my side of the car, and Philip can have his side how he wants it. I can even warm up my car seat, and he can make his cool. Pretty awesome! Sometimes I wish life was full of his-and-her every-thing, but it isn't. Most of the time, the conflict we experience in mar-riage arises because we are not willing to give up what we want.

I have a friend who was raised in a family whose way to resolve any conflict was to fight it out. Just fight until you win. Not necessarily physically fight, but definitely verbal fights that got louder and louder. One person always had to win, and the other was made to feel totally wrong. There was either complete domination or complete submission—no compromising or meeting in the middle.

Surely this is not the best way.

I have also talked to people raised in families where one of the parents always backed down from anything resembling a confronta-tion. One or both parents just gave in, to avoid any conflict whatso-ever. One of my friends, who grew up in this environment, said this method of resolving conflict kept the peace for a while, but that even-tually there was an inevitable explosion.

This way can't be good either.

There are right and wrong ways to face and resolve conflict.

I am not a big fan of boxing, but I do know that there are rules in boxing. In karate, there are rules. In wrestling, there are rules. I am not sure about the WWF or *lucha libre* (made famous in the movie *Nacho Libre*), but I suspect that, even in those matches, there are rules of some kind.

The first rule of conflict in marriage is to make sure that you are, personally, at peace with God. It sounds so basic. We are created to have a relationship with God, and all of our abilities to connect with people come out of our relationship with Him. I don't think that we can ever have peace with people if we haven't made our peace with God. Sometimes conflict occurs because we are expecting people—in this case, our spouse—to meet needs that only God can meet. We explored this idea more deeply in an earlier chapter. As amazing as Philip is—and he is amazing—he is not my Savior. He has nothing with which to save me. I must make peace with God rather than expecting Philip to make everything okay.

And out of our relationship with God, we need to talk to Him about whatever issue or conflict we are dealing with—the children, work, finances, whatever. Even the simple things, but especially those conflicts that you think might get a little heated. Talk to God about it *first. Pray first.* I wasn't always great at this; or, if I did talk to God about the problem, it was more like whining. Something like, "You made this lunatic I am married to . . . *You* fix him!" That is not the talking-to-God I am talking about.

Ask God just how much of the problem might be your fault. Before you attack or accuse or blame, check yourself out. Jesus said that before we worry about that little piece of sawdust in somebody else's eye, we should remove the tree trunk from our own. And we *all* have tree trunks in our own eyes sometimes. Yet we can get so focused on the weaknesses and faults of the other that we forget we have them. The reality is that whatever part of the conflict is my fault is 100 percent my fault. I have to own that.

So now, I ask myself questions like, *Am I being oversensitive? Am I being insensitive? Am I being ungrateful or too demanding?* Oftentimes, if I am honest, the answer to one of those is yes. And I am 100 percent responsible for my part.

Here is the tough part. Apologize for your part of the problem first.

Get great at saying "I'm sorry."

Not "I'm sorry, but . . ."

Just "I'm sorry for being oversensitive" or too demanding or whatever.

I am sure he needs to apologize, too. He has a tree trunk in his eye, too. But you can only deal with you. Be 100-percent responsible for your part. Get great at saying "I'm sorry." Because maybe, just maybe, you are wrong in this instance.

Fresh Perspective

My eyes can only see in the direction I am facing. I can't see behind me unless I turn my head. There are people behind me who can tell me if my shirt is untucked or if there is a string hanging from the bottom of my skirt, but looking in the direction my eyes are facing is the only perspective I have.

Likewise, each of us can only see life from our own perspective. And that means we all have the potential to be wrong in any given situation. Maybe in this particular instance I am wrong. I could be—and the more I am willing to say, or even acknowledge that likelihood, the more I pave the way toward building trust. And trust is the goal.

Even at work or with friends, I have found that if someone is willing to admit a fault or a wrong, then that is a heart I can work with. That is a heart I can partner with. Too many times we think that saying "I am sorry" or "I am wrong" might make us look bad. No, it doesn't. It makes us look strong; it takes a strong person to look at herself and say, "I am so sorry; I was oversensitive in that moment."

Apologizing does not mean that the issue is over; it just means that there is now the right atmosphere for solving whatever the conflict is.

Trying to see an issue from the other's point of view is important. It is not always easy, because again, we only see life from our own perspective. A number of years ago, Philip and I were looking for a house. This was when I was still living under the illusion that all men knew how to fix things, or at least knew how to manage people who knew how to fix things. We walked into a house that was for sale. It was the funkiest house ever. I just loved it. It had a tree growing

right in the middle of it. The previous owner had begun some reno-
vations and had laid the groundwork for what I thought would be
the most amazing house ever.

As I walked around the house, I was saying things like, "We could
put this here, and do that there. In this room we could do this." But
as Philip walked through it, he saw all the work that would need to be
done—none of which he knew how to do. In his mind, he saw months
of sawdust, hammers and chaos.

As he let me know there was no way we were going to live in that
house, I got frustrated. I said things like, "Why do we always have to
do things your way? Why can't we have a house like this?"

I remember walking off by myself, taking a few deep breaths and
really trying to see it from his perspective. He wanted a home. A peaceful home. He had no idea how to create a peaceful home out of this
half-finished building. I saw the stress that even the thought of living
there gave him.

So we walked away from that house that needed lots of work,
and eventually moved into a beautiful home that only required us
to unpack our boxes and hang a lamp. Perfect! Working hard at trying to see the issue from his point of view helped resolve that particular conflict.

Time and Place

Pick a good time to resolve the issue. Timing is key. Take it from me:
On the way to your husband's birthday party is probably *not* the time
to let him know that he could stand to lose a few pounds. (Wish I
could tell you I learned that from a book!) Now, the issue might be a
fair one to bring up, but the timing is not good.

Maybe his mom just got diagnosed with Alzheimer's. This is not
the time to tell him you think he should read a book on parenting.
Again, the issue is a fair one to bring up . . . the timing is just wrong.

The book of Esther tells the story of an ordinary girl who chose
to live an extraordinary life. She was orphaned, was raised by her uncle and, as a Jew in Persia, was living in a community of marginalized
people. Ultimately, she was selected by the king to be his queen. What
a fairy tale! Esther was living on easy street. She could have just kicked
back and enjoyed her life of royalty and leisure—and she probably did

for a while. But then she found out that her husband's right-hand man had devised a plan to kill all of the Jews.

What was she going to do?

Her uncle told Esther that she had a responsibility to go to the king and ask him to override the evil man's plans. At first she was hesitant to do this, knowing that it could cost her life; anyone approaching the king uninvited could be put to death. But then she realized that maybe rescuing her people was the very reason she was entrusted with her royal position. Maybe being queen wasn't just so she could enjoy luxury. Maybe she was in this position so that she could be a part of ending injustice. (Just a side thought here: I think you have been entrusted with this time in history and with your royal position so that, like Esther, you can be a part of ending injustice.)

Esther made the decision to approach the king. He didn't kill her. In fact, he asked what he could do for her.

What's interesting to me is that rather than telling him then and there about the plot to kill her people, Esther asked her husband to a banquet that she would prepare. Why didn't she just bring up the issue? I guess there was something about the time that didn't seem right.

The king enjoyed himself at the banquet and once again asked Esther what he could do for her. She said that it would be great if he would come to another banquet the next night. What? Why didn't she just get to the point? I have no idea. But I think there must have been something about the timing.

At the banquet the next night, Esther told the king—very humbly yet directly—about the plot devised by his right-hand man to kill her and her people. The king was appalled, and did everything in his power to see that she and her people were protected.

The conflict was resolved.

Esther was sensitive to the timing involved in resolving the conflict. There were times she could have said something but didn't.

I am not sure why waiting was a better option.

But her example made me realize that, just because the issue I am dealing with is at the forefront of my mind, I still need to be sensitive about whether this is the right time to bring it up. The goal is to resolve the issue, not to create another one.

Timing is important in conflict resolution, and so is place. Running out the door on the way somewhere is probably not the right place to resolve anything. Neither of us will feel like we are being heard and both of us will feel like we need to hurry. The place to work out an issue is away from the telephone and other distractions.

The bed is probably not the place to work out the issue either, because any man left horizontal for long will start snoring. (I didn't learn this from a book either. When Philip fell asleep in the middle of my sharing of an issue, it just created another issue we needed to deal with!) And the truth is, I just don't want our bed to be a place of conflict. It should be a place for intimacy. I don't want to bring a fight there.

I am not opposed to you having a disagreement in front of your children, as long as it is not an intense one, it is handled appropriately and your children see you resolve the conflict in a mature way. If they only see you fight, slam doors and go your own way, then that is the picture they have of conflict. Too many times, parents have a full-on, fully engaged, inappropriate attacking fight in front of their children—and the children, understandably, are freaked out. They're watching the people whom they are supposed to look to for guidance, wisdom and strength totally lose it. And that is a very scary thing for children. Maybe the parents resolve it behind closed doors a few hours later, but that does not help the children.

Taking a walk can be a great place for Philip and me to resolve issues. Or over coffee at Starbucks. Or sitting by the beach. Or walking through the woods. Or at a park bench. You pick a place that works for you.

Rules of Engagement

So there is a time and a place . . . and there is a *how*.

Remember that the time and place we have set aside is to resolve the issue, so come ready to do that. This is not the time to blame. This is not about *his* problem or *my* problem. We are married. This is *our* problem. We are on the same team. Sometimes, in the middle of a heated conflict, it is easy to forget that and to begin to point fingers.

Often, Philip and I don't see eye to eye. (By now, this is probably not a surprise to you.) But we are both committed to working out this problem together. Some days, it is messier than others.

In films, I have heard a soldier ask his superior officer what the rules of this engagement are. In other words, how and with what weapons should we fight. In marriage conflicts, there must be rules of engagement. There are some very basic rules, ones you probably learned in kindergarten: No yelling. No pushing. No hitting. No kicking. No biting. No slamming doors.

In addition to those basics, I am going to give you a few of ours; you can feel free to use these or come up with your own. Whatever you decide, it is important that you and your spouse agree on them, so that in the heat of the moment, you don't go with what you're feeling, but stick to the rules you have decided on together.

Watch That Mouth!

Let no foul or polluting language, nor evil word nor unwholesome or worthless talk [ever] come out of your mouth, but only such [speech] as is good and beneficial to the spiritual progress of others, as is fitting to the need and the occasion, that it may be a blessing and give grace (God's favor) to those who hear it.

Let all bitterness and indignation and wrath (passion, rage, bad temper) and resentment (anger, animosity) and quarreling (brawling, clamor, contention) and slander (evil-speaking, abusive or blasphemous language) be banished from you, with all malice (spite, ill will, or baseness of any kind).

And become useful and helpful and kind to one another, tenderhearted (compassionate, understanding, loving-hearted), forgiving one another [readily and freely], as God in Christ forgave you (Eph. 4:29,31-32).

Think about the damage before you launch that verbal missile. Sadly, sometimes my method is *Ready... Fire... Aim.* Not good, and it can cause damage impossible to fix. Words cannot be taken back, only forgiven.

I love M&Ms, especially the peanut ones. Back when I used to eat that kind of stuff, I could eat one bag in about 35 seconds—35 seconds to polish off a bag of fat, sugar and calories and about 30 minutes of exercise to work it off. Not to mention the hours that my body required to get rid of the toxins in it.

This is like a verbal missile: We can throw a hurtful word in a matter of seconds, but it may take years to work it off.

There once was a little boy who had a bad temper. His father gave him a bag of nails and told him that every time he lost his temper, he must hammer a nail into the back of the fence.

The first day the boy had driven 37 nails into the fence. Over the next few weeks, as he learned to control his anger, the number of nails hammered daily gradually dwindled down.

He discovered it was easier to hold his temper than to drive those nails into the fence.

Finally the day came when the boy didn't lose his temper at all. He told his father about it; and the father suggested that the boy now pull out one nail for each day that he was able to hold his temper.

The days passed and the young boy was finally able to tell his father that all the nails were gone.

The father took his son by the hand and led him to the fence. He said, "You have done well, my son, but look at the holes in the fence. The fence will never be the same. When you say things in anger, they leave a scar just like this one. You can put a knife in a man and draw it out. It won't matter how many times you say I'm sorry, the wound is still there." A verbal wound is as bad as a physical one.[1]

Most of the time we are kinder and more polite to strangers and acquaintances than we are to our spouse. It should not be that way, but often it is. Little acts of kindness can go a long way toward diffusing conflict. I never feel like being courteous or kind when Philip and I are disagreeing; I feel like criticizing, blaming and generally being anything but kind. If I do choose to be kind or courteous, the conflict can be diffused. I can throw water or oil on the flame. It is up to me.

There are some verbal weapons that Philip and I have agreed will never be launched. We have decided that no matter what kind of conflict we get into, we would never use the word "divorce." Ever. If divorce is not an option, then working the conflict out is the only solution.

We try to refrain from using words like "never" and "always," because they are rarely true. "You *never* do anything I want to do!" "You *always* ignore me!" "You *never* think of me!" "You *never* say that you love me!"

Nobody "always" or "never" does anything, so be careful about using these absolute words.

It is better to express feelings using the expression "I feel . . ."

"I feel lonely or worried when you don't call me on the phone."

"I feel hurt when you talk about me to other people."

"I feel sad when you ignore me."

And, it is important to note that we each own our own feelings; the other person is not responsible. Using the expression "I feel . . ." is better than "you made me feel . . ." because nobody can *make* you feel anything.

Seek Good Counsel

Often in the middle of a disagreement or conflict with our spouse, we talk to others about it. That can be a good thing; it depends on who you are talking to.

I knew a woman who was having some serious marriage issues (we all do from time to time). I found out that she was spending quite a bit of her time with a group of girlfriends who had either been divorced a few times, were angry at men or were determined never to get married. What advice could this particular group of women give her that would be helpful? They said things to her like, "Just leave him. You are smarter and more capable than him." These weren't bad women; they were just not able to give her any tools for navigating the particular challenge she was in. They could not help her stay married in the face of the challenge she and her spouse were facing.

Get help when you need it, but make sure you are getting help from people who are further up the road from you. If you want to build a successful business, get advice from someone who has done it. If you want to play an instrument, get lessons from someone who can play. If you want to build a marriage, get input from people who are doing it well: happily married people who have the kind of relationship you would like to have.

Think Straight

Sometimes in the middle of conflict, I have to remind myself of Philip's good qualities. It is easy to get distracted by the annoying things; the annoying things are annoying. So many times, the annoying

things scream louder than the good qualities, so we have to intentionally concentrate on the good on purpose.

Just recently, I was *so* irritated with Philip. Nothing major—just
everything he did or didn't do bothered me. So then that triggered
lots of thoughts, mostly about his weaknesses. I found myself
dwelling on his weaknesses. Not good.

I spend time every day reading the Bible and praying, and on this
day I felt like God said to me, "Holly, stop it. Take those thoughts cap-
tive. They are not producing anything good. Think on some things
that are great about Philip." Well, it took some time. I wasn't so willing to quit my mental Philip bashing. But I did. It took me a minute
to think of one thing I liked about him. One thing. That was all I
could come up with for a while. Then one more.

Paul challenged the Philippians to look for the best in each other,
and when we do that, then God will work into us "his most excellent
harmony."

> Summing it all up, friends, I'd say you'll do best by filling
> your minds and meditating on things true, noble, reputable,
> authentic, compelling, gracious—*the best, not the worst; the beau-*
> *tiful, not the ugly; things to praise, not things to curse.* Put into prac-
> tice what you learned from me, what you heard and saw and
> realized. Do that, and God, who makes everything work to-
> gether, will work you into *his most excellent harmonies* (Phil. 4:8,
> *THE MESSAGE*, emphasis added).

Conflict resolution.

Nobody said it would be easy.

And countless marriages fail because neither one wants to learn
how to resolve the conflicts. If you leave this marriage thinking that
the problem was just him, I would like to suggest that you will have
conflicts in the next marriage, too.

Because two becoming one is not always a smooth process, you
might as well learn some of the tools now. In the corporate and legal
worlds, people are paid a lot of money to help resolve conflicts. You
won't get the big bucks for resolving conflicts in marriage, but you
will have the opportunity to build a lifelong partnership that is strong
and lasting.

Weathering the Storms

There are conflicts that arise in a marriage because of storms on the outside. Pervasive attitudes in our culture are an example. I actually believe that the pressure on our marriages is much more severe than it was for our parents. The media certainly isn't helping either. How many happy (and not dysfunctional!!) two-parent families do you see portrayed on television?

Humanism

The desire to put *me* first is a prevalent theme in our society today. We can't be foolish and think that it won't affect us. Plenty of marriages end because one or both spouses have succumbed to the humanistic thought pattern of *I will do whatever is good for me, regardless of what my desires do to our marriage*. We might not say that out loud—it might be underneath our actions. This is the if-it-feels-good-do-it mentality, and it will destroy a marriage. *We* always has to be more important than *me* if a marriage is going to weather the storms of life.

Materialism

The quest for more and more stuff is another external pressure that can damage a marriage. We become so focused on working hard so that we can gather things that we end up having less time to spend together. The media, in a not-so-subtle way, convinces us that the more stuff we have, the happier we'll be.

"This house isn't big enough; we need a bigger one."

"This car isn't new; we need a new one."

"My clothes are soooo last season; I need more."

Now, I am not saying that we can't have a nice home, car or clothes. I am saying, look at the cost. If you have to work three jobs or a job that requires 80 hours a week in order to pay for all of the newer and better stuff, connecting with each other will be hard. And if you can make time for connection after that 80-hour workweek, chances are high that you or your spouse will be too exhausted or irritated to enjoy one another.

Materialism says, "Stuff is more important than relationships." Again, most of us would say that we don't believe that, but how are we living? Many times what we say we believe does not line up with our actions. J. Paul Getty was the wealthiest man in the world during his lifetime. He said, "I would give my entire fortune for one happy marriage." If you spend more time maintaining your lifestyle than maintaining your marriage, then the lack of intimacy and connection may cost you the relationship.

The Importance of Resiliency

Other storms can attack a marriage. These are the crises that come upon most of us at one time or another. We will all face a crisis we did not anticipate, that we feel unprepared for. Some of us will face losing a job, a bankruptcy, a lawsuit, a natural disaster, the death of a parent, the death of a child, loss of friends, being disabled, getting a life-threatening disease . . . and the list goes on. When the worst happens, marriages whose foundations are already shaky and uncertain often crumble under the pressure.

After 9/11, our initial instinct as a nation and as families was to draw closer together. But as the initial shock wore off, some marriages were unable to survive. Delayed trauma and feelings of despair can shift our world. This was especially true for those who were directly affected by the tragedy or were involved in the rescue operations. Years later, we have seen a sharp rise in divorce among firefighters and police whose lives were forever altered by the loss of colleagues, family members and friends.

In weathering the storms that come against a marriage, we need to be resilient people. We can't be so frail or so rigid that storms can destroy us.

Palm trees are so resilient that in a storm they will not break, but instead bend to the earth. After the storm, they rise to their former state and continue their growth.

Buildings in Southern California, where I live, are built to withstand a great shaking. From new houses to the tallest Los Angeles skyscrapers, architects and builders have incorporated various designs and materials to help the buildings stand strong through earthquakes. Outside forces necessitate offices and dwellings built with resiliency.

Jesus told us to build our houses . . . our lives . . . on a rock, a firm foundation. If we do that, then when the storms of life come, we might sway a little, but we won't be destroyed.

Some people appear to have a special capacity for optimism and resilience, while others are easily driven to despair when the balance of their lives is upset. Resilient people survive and even thrive in the face of struggle. Resilient couples are more likely to weather the large and small storms of life better than those couples who are fearful and unsteady.[2]

In order to keep together through the crisis, remember that *we* is very important. Together *we* are stronger. Together *we* can get through this.

Don't isolate. You need each other. Don't blame. Blame separates. It was not Philip's fault that I got cancer. It was not my fault. It just happened. Our marriage is different today because we had to navigate this crisis. We didn't handle it perfectly; we just handled it together. There were times when I made so many diet and health changes in one day that Philip's head was spinning—and he was just a bit frustrated. There were times when he was not as conscious of what I was feeling as I would have liked. Regardless, we got through it together. There were some messy moments, but we are stronger today.

(By the way, I am five years cancer-free. YEA!!!)

Keeping a sense of humor is crucial for dealing with the crises that come. After the devastation of the 1994 earthquake in Los Angeles that caused severe damage in our home (our house cracked rather than swayed!), I remember Philip looking at the piles of shattered china on our kitchen floor and commenting, "Well, you said you wanted new dishes. Now I believe you!" We laughed for a moment and then began the long process of cleaning up. And we didn't stay at the cleanup process all day either. We took our kids, drove to a hotel in another county (one where the earth wasn't moving!) and got in a Jacuzzi. We took a few moments amid the crisis to make some fun. It helped.

Don't let the crisis separate you. Don't let the plans of the enemy bring division. Work through the crisis together.

Two are better than one,
because they have a good return for their work:
If one falls down,
his friend can help him up.
But pity the man who falls
and has no one to help him up!
Also, if two lie down together, they will keep warm.
But how can one keep warm alone?

Though one may be overpowered,
two can defend themselves.
A cord of three strands is not quickly broken.
ECCLESIASTES 4:9-12, *NIV*

Seasons Change

Every marriage goes through different seasons. Some are more fun than others! Each season comes with its own rewards and challenges.

In the beginning of a marriage, while it is certainly still "the honeymoon," there is an adjustment needed as you each learn that you can't do what you want to do when you want to do it. There are now two of you. Someone else to consider. No longer a season of singleness, but togetherness. New season.

Many of us have or will have children. Wow, they change your world, don't they? When our son, Jordan, was born, we were of course thrilled. He was loved and welcomed. I just don't think we were prepared for the time, energy and stuff that come with a baby. Is anyone? Living on little sleep and often not much time together took its toll on our marriage. We had to work through that season. Then a few years later, along came our daughter. Even more juggling. Trying to find time together became very difficult, so again we had to make the time. We scheduled dates. If our marriage was going to make it through the baby and toddler phases, we were going to have to find the time to spend together—as Philip and Holly, not just Daddy and Mommy.

Then there are seasons when your job might require lots of your time. That's great, as long as the two of you are communicating about it. About 15 years ago, I began to travel around the world speaking. This was a new season for us. At the beginning, it was a bit messy. I scheduled too many trips back to back with not enough breathing room in the middle. The traveling was fine—we both believed it was what God had for me—but we needed to schedule it so that it would work with our family and my responsibilities at our home church, the Oasis. No problem . . . just a new season that had to be navigated. It would have become a problem if we weren't talking about it and figuring it out together.

Many of us have had or will have teenagers in our homes. Exciting time of life, isn't it? I love that my children are becoming my friends. It is so encouraging to watch them walk out their own relationships with Jesus and discover what God put them on the planet to fulfill. It is a great season that comes with its own challenges. Teens stay up late, so finding time for Philip and me to have our own intimate time became tricky. I had to get over being embarrassed that they knew what was going on behind the closed door—when they were little, they went to bed before us, so it hadn't been an issue. Just another season of life! As teenagers they were given more responsibility, including a car. That certainly helped with the errands . . . but, at the same time, it made us pray more! Navigating the emotions of teenage girls can be tricky. I actually think I handle it more easily than Philip, but it has taken both of us, encouraging each other along the way, to get through this season. Remember, you are on the same team!

What about the empty nest season? I am almost there—and I am looking forward to it. I love my children, but I am going to love the time Philip and I will have together. It will be awesome!

I am not sure Philip and I will ever retire (not sure how to retire from building God's kingdom!), but I imagine that our daily work life will change. That will be a new season to look forward to and to negotiate.

And how about the grandparent season?

The great-grandparent season?

Determining to handle the seasons of life together will make all the difference in getting through them. You are in this together, for the long haul!

And when you think about it, in spite of the conflicts, two really are better than one. In so many ways . . . from handling serious situations to everyday mundane things.

When ordering at a restaurant, you can share two dinners. You get the salad and he orders the BBQ chicken. Perfect. Now he can have some salad and you get some chicken. Two are better than one.

When at the grocery store, one of you can get in the long line while the other races to get the last two items. Two are better than one.

When entering the lodge after a long day snow skiing, he can order your hot drink while you are still trying to get your skis off. Two are better than one.

When attempting to zip up a dress that might require you to dislocate your shoulder, he walks up and does it effortlessly. Two are better than one.

Talk . . . Listen . . . Talk . . . Listen

Deficient or failed communication is often listed as a reason for divorce. I actually think that lack of communication is *the* number-one reason for a broken marriage. Even if a couple says that their divorce was due to disagreements about finances or irreconcilable differences or even infidelity, I believe that any area of challenge could be overcome with better communication. If a couple has trouble with their finances and it produces stress, but they are great at talking about it, communicating will go a long way toward resolving that issue.

Communication is key.

The word "communication" comes from the Latin word *communis*, which means "to make common." Basically, communication is *making common* the needs, desires, thoughts and feelings of our hearts, so that both parties can understand each other.

Communication is more than verbal. Our expressions, our body language, the look in our eyes and our tone often have as much an impact—sometimes more—than our words. If you say "I love you" while looking into the eyes of your spouse in a gentle tone with a soft touch, the words are more believable than if you say them begrudgingly and looking away.

Same words. Different body language.

When it comes to communication, it all matters.

Saying "I'm sorry" is important in a marriage. Saying it sincerely and looking at your spouse when you do communicates the apology you want. Saying it reluctantly while looking down does not come across as a sincere apology. We often trust the accuracy of non-verbal behaviors more than the words themselves. Again, the content is good, but the context in which the words are said is equally important.

Communication is the exchange and flow of information and ideas from one person to another. It involves a sender transmitting an idea, a thought or information to a receiver. Effective communication occurs *only* if the receiver understands the exact information or idea that the sender intended to transmit. Therein lies the problem.

We think we have communicated something just because we have said it, but as Freeman Teague, Jr. once said, "Nothing is so simple that it cannot be misunderstood."

Often we don't communicate what we want to say; we might think we know what we are saying, but what we think we are saying is not what comes across.

Philip is a fan of The Beatles. When we were planning our annual GodChicks conference, he mentioned to me that he thought we should do one of their songs. I said, "Great, I will find one that will fit."

He said, "I have an idea for one." When I asked him which one, he said the song "Something." We listened to the song, and at first it seemed awesome. But then, right after the man in the song communicated his love and admiration for the woman, he made the comment about not being sure whether their love would grow or not.

Uhhhh . . . this is not good. At least, it is not good if you are trying to communicate commitment and a forever love! We decided not to use that song because it did not say what we wanted to communicate.

The apostle Paul wrote to the church in Corinth about another difficult aspect of communication: "Oh, dear Corinthian friends! We have spoken honestly with you, and our hearts are open to you. There is no lack of love on our part, but you have withheld your love from us. I am asking you to respond as if you were my own children. Open your hearts to us!" (2 Cor. 6:11-13, NLT). In his letter, Paul is saying that he has spoken honestly and freely to them. His heart has been open, yet they have not reciprocated. He has been willing to communicate, but they have not.

In becoming better at communication in your marriage, you need to be willing. Be someone who is willing to open up. Be someone who will attempt to express the thoughts of your heart.

Philip will never know me, and we will never experience real intimacy, if I do not share the feelings, thoughts and ideas in my heart. The trick for me is being clear in what I am expressing. Am I saying what I think I am saying?

On the flip side, am I creating an atmosphere in which he feels safe to open up to me? His opening up cannot be forced, but I can do my part to create an atmosphere that makes it easy. Asking him for advice is one way to get him to open up: "What do you think about this situation?" Even if I think I know all the answers (I never do), I still ask what he thinks. The goal is to create an open atmosphere, not to prove someone right or wrong.

Another way I have found to open Philip up is to express an interest in something he is interested in.

Philip is a serious Yankee fan. Just ask how much Yankee stuff he has.

T-shirts.

Jerseys.

Coats.

Jackets.

Caps.

Watches.

Pictures.

Snow globes.

Beanies.

No kidding. He has the MLB application on his iPhone just so he can keep up with the Yankee games. He can be anywhere, turn on the app and watch those Yankees. Yippee. We manage to make it to New York City a few times each year; and interesting enough, it is always during baseball season. Because I love my husband, I have become a Yankee fan (though I am managing to be a fan without all the paraphernalia or the iPhone app).

If Philip has had a bad day, or is frustrated dealing with different issues and seems to be a little closed off, I can get him to open up if I start talking about baseball. If I start asking questions about Derek Jeter or A-Rod, or about how many games ahead of the Boston Red Sox the Yankees are, within 10 minutes he is a different person. All I did was show a bit of interest in something he is interested in.

Philip does the same for me. And occasionally I tell him the long version of what I am thinking, but mainly I stick to the streamlined version, so that I can finish before his eyes start to glaze over.

Philip's parents were divorced when he was quite young. It was not a quiet, amicable divorce (I'm not sure how many of those there are). His parents fought, yelled, blamed each other and were so loud that the police were called. In fact, the police came to their house so many times that Philip knew the officers by name. As a child, he experienced communication at its worst. Nobody was honoring, nobody was listening, nobody was creating a safe place for the family.

Philip's personality, as I mentioned before, is fairly introverted. He is someone who processes things within. Because of his background and his quiet personality, he has every excuse to be a poor communicator. And yet, when we were dating, he was the one asking questions. He would ask me things like, "What do you think your strengths are? What are three things you wish I would talk to you about? What do you think my strengths are?"

He was creating an atmosphere where feelings and thoughts could be expressed. Based on where he came from, this doesn't seem like it would come naturally, yet his desire was to head the opposite direction from where he'd come. He wanted to become an effective communicator.

Perhaps just as important as expressing our thoughts clearly and creating an atmosphere for open communication is listening.

Hearing and *listening* are not the same thing. Hearing is the act of perceiving sound. It simply refers to the reception of aural stimuli, which is involuntary.

Listening, on the other hand, is a selective activity that involves the reception and the interpretation of aural stimuli. It involves decoding the sound into meaning.

Listening is divided into two main categories: *passive* and *active*. Passive listening is little more than hearing. It occurs when the receiver of the message has little motivation to listen carefully, such as when listening to music, storytelling and television or when being polite.

People generally speak at 100 to 175 words per minute (according to the people in my world, I speak about twice that fast!), but they can listen intelligently at 600 to 800 WPM. Because only a part of our mind has to pay attention to so few words, it is easy to go into "mind drift"—thinking about other things while listening to someone. The cure for this is active listening, which involves listening with a purpose. It requires that the listener attend to the words and the feelings of the sender for understanding. It takes the same amount or more energy than speaking. It requires the receiver to hear the various messages, understand the meaning and then verify the meaning by offering feedback.[3]

If we are going to be great at communicating in our marriage—if we are going to be great at resolving conflict—we must become active listeners. The apostle James offers us the recipe for great active listening: "Everyone should be quick to listen, slow to speak and slow to become angry" (Jas. 1:19, *NIV*). Active listeners spend more time listening than talking. (I fail at this sometimes.) Active listeners do not just appear to listen while actually waiting for a break in the conversation to say what they want to say. (I fail at this sometimes, too.) Active listeners maintain eye contact, make encouraging noises that let the talker know he is being heard—noises like "Hmmm . . . really . . . wow . . ."—and often take notes.

I have learned the benefits of notetaking. Once Philip decides to share something, he does not like to be interrupted with questions. I like it when he interrupts me with questions, because it lets me know he is listening—but that is just another way men and women are different! Philip does not like the interruptions because he won't remember where he was in the conversation. So I write down my thoughts or questions and express them later.

Effective communication is a learned skill. We can all get better at opening up, at talking and at really listening. And we must. If our marriages are going to make it through the conflicts that inevitably arise from inside and outside, we must become stronger communicators.

For some more help with navigating conflict, check out a short video from Philip and me at www.godchicks.com.

Just for the Men!

There are right and wrong ways to face and resolve conflict.

Fighting to the death verbally or physically is not the way. Total domination or complete submission should not be our only options in resolving conflict. Nor is holding and repressing tension or frustration until massive blowout a good way to handle our disagreements.

We must be willing to fight fair, to work toward compromise and to take divorce off the table. If divorce is not an option, we will work together toward solutions.

Build a strong foundation.

Think about a general contractor. When he constructs a massive building, he doesn't start building on the asphalt or grass. He has to gut out the ground and make a solid foundation. Jesus tells us to build our house (our life) on the rock, which is Him, so that when storms come, the wind and the weather may beat on the house but they cannot take it down. If we build our house on asphalt or grass or sand, as Jesus says, it won't take much stormy weather to completely destroy it.

Build well.

Crises will come. Remember that *we* is most important.

Cancer strikes. Family members pass away. A job loss occurs. A fire, earthquake or tornado leaves you with almost nothing. Now is the time to draw closer together than ever. Determine to weather this season together. Inject humor when you can. Encourage and support one another. Keep loving, even when it is hard, by making time to connect and build intimacy.

Communication is key.

Communicating clearly through the storms is wise. It is also necessary. Three things to remember when communicating: *time, place* and *how*.

Choose to dialogue about difficult issues at the right time, so that both you and your spouse have the mental capacity to stay as levelheaded as possible.

Choose the right place, so that you will be heard without frustrating your partner.

Consider how you speak when confronting one another. Tone and body language are often more powerful than words. Mean what you say with your tone and with your body. Effective communication is not that you spoke, but that you were heard.

Notes

1. Anonymous, "The Too True Story of the Nail in the Fence."
2. Dr. Robin Smith, *Lies at the Altar: The Truth About Great Marriages* (New York: Hyperion, 2004), p. 90.
3. Donald Clark, "Communication and Leadership," updated May 2008. http://www.nwlink.com/~Donclark/leader/leadcom.html (accessed December 2009).

8

Purpose-Driven Wife

(Philip)

*One thing I know: the only ones among you who will be really happy
are those who have sought and found how to serve.*
ALBERT SCHWEITZER

An excellent wife [a wife of valor] is the crown of her husband.
PROVERBS 12:4, NKJV

"It's not about you."

Okay, that has been used before. But it's especially true if you
want to build a thriving marriage. Marriage flourishes when your focus is on serving your spouse, empowering him to love life and sup-
porting him in reaching his God-given dreams. In every relationship,
your focus should be to encourage others to pursue their God-given
destiny and inspire them to endure life's setbacks—but especially in
your relationship with your spouse.

It's not about you.

Marriage is *not* about me reaching my goals first "because I'm the
man." Marriage *is* about me, as the husband/leader, encouraging and
inspiring my wife to fulfill God's purpose for her life. That's also the
attitude I expect from her toward me. We both need to have the
other's best interests at heart.

Whether God's purpose for my wife is to be an amazing mom for
our children, a successful businesswoman or a leader in the community, achieving it is an important issue to Him and a key to fulfillment
for her. That means her purpose needs to be important to me, too.

You Have a Purpose

Women, you have a destiny! Every individual has a destiny. It's important that you pursue God's purpose for your life. It can be a great help to be inspired by others whom you are watching as they honor God and thrive in their life. But don't compare yourself to them too closely... God has something unique for you, a unique and irreplaceable purpose for you. I believe God desires us all to fulfill our destiny. My desire is to encourage and support you in becoming all God called you to be.

In a book written by John and Stasi Eldredge titled *Captivating,* I read some important insights into the soul of a woman. (The subtitle of the book is "Unveiling the Mystery of a Woman's Soul.") One of the interesting things the Eldredges say about women is:

> Every woman I've ever met feels something deeper than just the sense of failing at what she does. An underlying, gut feeling of failing at who she is. It's that feeling of "I'm not enough," and "I am too much" all at the same time.
>
> I'm not pretty enough. I'm not thin enough. I'm not kind enough, not gracious enough, not disciplined enough. But too emotional, too needy, too sensitive, too strong, too opinionated, too messy.[1]

Many women are asking themselves the question, *Who am I supposed to be?* John and Stasi Eldredge tell us that women wonder, "Is a true woman Cinderella, Joan of Arc, Mary Magdalene, or Oprah?"[2] *What is my role? Who am I trying to be?*

Often the message expressed to women, even by the church, leaves them feeling as though they're not the women they ought to be. It is not surprising that many men pull away from the deeper waters of a woman's soul, unsure about what he might find and wondering if he can handle it. But our job is to honor the women in our life and, by our support, override the message so many women have accepted, a message that has left them uninspired and devalued.

When I read about the "Proverbs 31 Woman," I can understand how it can feel like biblical proof to many women that they just don't measure up! The Proverbs 31 woman is like super woman. I mean, she does it all and does it great. That woman is *busy*. How does she do it? When does she have time to read books, have a hobby, exercise, hang out with her friends or have sex with her husband?[3] There is no room in this girl's schedule. The light never goes out! She's working hard, multi-tasking, in bed at midnight and up at 4:00 A.M.!

Her example can lead to more questions, instead of answers:

What is a good woman?

How do I become a strong woman without being harsh?

How do I express vulnerability without drowning myself in my emotions?

Does God have a purpose for me that is significant?

Women put so much value in the relationships in their life, and the voice of a "significant man" in a woman's life can have tremendous influence in providing the deeply felt answers to these questions. Men's words can have a tremendous impact. For this reason, it is important for a woman to be cautious in determining which males have access to her heart.

Letting the man in your life know the importance of his words can help him see the impact he has and what you need him to do when it comes to speaking "words of life." I see women everywhere who are waiting for the significant men in their lives to say in an empowering way:

"I'm proud of you."

"You are important to me."

"I believe in you."

"Is there anything I can do to help you succeed?"

"You've got something valuable to offer to our world."

My Role

Everyone loves a love story.

I have watched *Sleepless in Seattle* at least 10 times. I've watched *Notting Hill*, *The American President* and *Ever After* about 8 times each.

The girls in my life love these movies. So we watch.

Little did I know, when I was watching *Little Mermaid* with my little girl, how much I would relate to the dad trying to protect his "little mermaid" from her own dangerous decisions.

I have a responsibility to help write my daughter's future. I have also come to realize that, in many ways, I also hold the pen of God's effort to write an amazing story in Holly's life.

The apostle Peter gives me some instruction about how to do this well: "Husbands, in the same way be considerate as you live with your wives and treat them with respect as the weaker partner and as heirs with you of the gracious gift of life, so that nothing will hinder your prayers" (1 Pet. 3:7, *NIV*). I must recognize my wife as an heir with me of the gift of life. I want my prayers to be effective and to have power, and I risk that when I ignore the principle of this Scripture. No one wants to bring a hindering element into his or her prayer. If I don't excel at honoring my wife and seeing us as heirs together in the gracious gift of life, I can hinder our faith—I can totally miss out on God's blessing.

My support, endorsement and involvement have massive impact on the lives of my wife and daughter. Both the subtle messages and the grand gestures are huge, but I too easily forget how significant my contribution is. Think of Clark Kent—you know, the mild-mannered reporter who has super powers. Imagine that Clark wakes up one morning and forgets that he is Superman. He walks through his morning routine but forgets to hold back a bit so that his strength doesn't do any damage. He slams the door a bit too hard and it comes off the hinges. He puts his coffee mug down and it breaks off at the handle. He pushes the toaster switch down and the whole thing falls apart. He wonders to himself, *Why is everything so fragile?* He's unaware of his own strength and assumes the problem must lie with the items he has broken. He is surprised at the impact his actions produce, and he leaves a trail of destruction all through his home.[4]

Too many men don't know their own strength. They say insensitive things, leave out compliments, issue criticisms and point out flaws in the women they love—leaving a trail of brokenness in their wake. And all the time they wonder, *Why is she so fragile?*

One day I will stand before God. One thing I do not want to hear from Him is, "What have you been doing? I had this amazing woman walking through life with you, lying right next to you in bed and sitting right next to you at the dinner table, but you didn't allow her to flourish. You didn't inspire her. You didn't value the gift inside her. She was part of your assignment. But you always put yourself first. She was the key to much of the success I had planned for you. But because of your selfishness, she has become the key to your lack of success."

When the Bible tells us that husbands are the "head" of the marriage, it does not mean that men are the bosses or that everything is to be done our way. It means that we are responsible for inspiring our family and for leading them in such a way that they live out God's plan for their lives. The success or failure of a company lies with the leadership of the CEO. The success or failure of a church lies with the leadership of the pastor. And the success or failure of a marriage and both spouses lies with the leadership of the husband. God will hold me accountable for the "man-made ceilings" I erect over the lives of the women in my world.

The attitude of some men is, "My goals are most important. If I reach my goals and we have time and money left over, we'll try to pursue some of her goals." But if I only focus on myself as the priority, I limit the potential of other family members—and eventually my own. My leadership should create an environment in which those who love me flourish.

Jules Ormont said, "A great leader never sets himself above his followers except in carrying responsibilities."[5] I must ask myself, *Are the dreams in the heart of my wife stolen by yielding to my leadership, or are they thriving?*

I think God will look at me one day and ask questions:

"Did you help bring out My purpose in your wife's life?"

"Did you encourage her gifts and abilities?"

"Did you set her up to win, or did your insecurities and traditions keep you from allowing her to fulfill My plan for her life?"

Author Keith Ferrazzi writes, "Human ambitions are like Japanese carp; they grow proportional to the size of their environment."[6] I believe that it's my job to create an environment in our home that is big enough for Holly to reach her purpose.

I used to love watching Phil Jackson coach Michael Jordan and the Chicago Bulls. What a team! They turned each other into heroes. In their best moments, they did not compete against each other; they worked together to achieve what they could never do on their own. I'm sure they had their disagreements and personal battles, as any relationship has, but the overriding foundation of their relationship was to bring out the best in the other.

I see the husband-wife relationship as very similar. My job, as husband, is to set up my wife to succeed. It is my goal to see her succeeding, to see her fulfilled . . . to see her become a champion. We work together. We cause each other to succeed.

I'm Coach Phil. She's MJ.

If she wins, we all win.

If I am a winner, she's a winner.

If Coach Phil and MJ had continual disagreements—"This is *my* team!" "No, it's *my* team!" "What about me? I want to be the leader!!" "I'm the coach, so what I say goes"—they likely would not have gotten very far. Many teams with great potential are destroyed by petty selfishness and misunderstandings about roles.

What if one of my main jobs as a husband and father is to ensure the success of the girls in my life? Is it possible that this is my commission? Every woman has a calling in life, and that calling or purpose is just as important as a man's. God desires that we all fulfill our destiny, and that not one fulfills their purpose at the expense of the other.

Jesus told us that "greater love has no one than this, that he lay down his life for his friends" (John 15:13, *NIV*). Wouldn't it be great if husbands and wives were willing to lay down their lives for each other?

Somebody's Little Girl

It's hard to explain the heart of a dad. The sense of responsibility is unparalleled. It doesn't really matter how old my daughter gets or how successful she may be in our world, she will always be "my little girl." Having a daughter can inspire in a man a tremendous sense of wanting to protect and to love and, at the same time, a weird fear of being absolutely inadequate for the task.

I looked at the world with different eyes when we had a daughter. I got a new look at the world. And as a dad, there are four things that drive my heart when I think of my daughter:

1. I want to encourage her to be all that she can be in this life.
2. I want to provide every opportunity for her to pursue her heart's desire.
3. I want to protect her from anything that would harm her.
4. I want her to know that I love her like no one else.

I recently saw the movie *Taken,* which is about a young teenage girl captured in Europe by a gang of men who intend to sell her into the sex trade. A few weeks after we saw the movie, my daughter, Paris, was preparing to leave the country. Although she has traveled to many different nations, I told her, "Paris, when you are traveling, be careful—be alert and pay attention to what's going on around you. I am not Liam Neeson. I have no special skills! I am not Jason Bourne. I'm more like . . . Clark Kent, but without the super powers. I'm just Philip, your dad. Please protect yourself when I am not there to do it."

The global sex trade is a growing threat to women, but it is not the only one. It is disturbing to me when women are demeaned or relegated to sex objects by our society. Often, singers, songwriters and advertisers are guilty of this easy sell. While many people tolerate this and even celebrate the disgusting "craft" of making girls into objects of pleasure in general, I get angry. When I see a battered woman, a drug addict or homeless woman, I think, *There is somebody's little girl. How would I act or treat her if she were my little girl?*

Every race of people has experienced prejudice of some kind in their history. Blacks were bought and sold as slaves for many centuries. The original residents of the Americas were slaughtered or pushed out of their native lands. Jews have been persecuted in every place and time they have lived. Arabic peoples have endured unfair suspicion and stereotyping, especially since 9/11. The list goes on and on.

But I believe that no people group has experienced oppression like women—oppression that has been accepted and even institutionalized since the beginning of recorded history. And it continues today. More girls died in the last 50 years simply because they were girls than men killed in all wars of the twentieth century.[7] This must break God's heart!

Global organizations have become aware in recent years of the need to equip and empower women: "There's a growing recognition among everyone from the World Bank to the U.S. military's Joint Chiefs of Staff to aid organizations like CARE that focusing on women and girls is the most effective way to fight global poverty and extremism. That's why foreign aid is increasingly directed to women. The world is awakening to a powerful truth: Women and girls aren't the problem; they're the solution."[8]

Every single woman is somebody's little girl.

I may not be able to do much for a woman halfway around the world, but I can make sure that the dreams in the hearts of my wife and daughter don't die. In the statistics mentioned above, it's notable that the countries where women are the most oppressed, uneducated and devalued are also the countries that have the highest rate of poverty and famine. Could it be that we are keeping our personal lives in some kind of poverty when we do not sufficiently love the women in our lives and honor their need to live out their purpose?

If my wife believes her main calling is to be at home to raise our children, I want to live my life in a way that gives her freedom to do that. I want to arrange our life, as best I can, so that we can afford that financially. I don't want to pressure her to go out and accomplish something that's not in her heart to do.

On the other hand, if my wife has ambitions in her heart that we believe to be God's purpose for her life, whether they are to achieve in the business world, in ministry or in other areas, I also want to live my life in a way that empowers her to pursue and achieve those ambitions. I promised, 25 years ago, to honor my wife in our marriage. In part, that means inspiring her to bring out her giftedness and pursue her passion while together we build a family. And while building a healthy family is one of our highest priorities, I believe we both may need to make sacrifices to see that Holly realizes her potential outside our home as well.

In the business world, we've made great strides in empowering women. Women's successes in the marketplace are worth celebrating, but it's shocking that there were "great strides" that needed to be made in the first place. And there is still more to do in terms of recognition, appreciation and respect for women in the workplace. We need to recognize their value, release their unique abilities and honor them.

Men have often dishonored—and therefore missed out on—the greatest gift in our life and world. It's the women around us.

Jesus, Women and Traditions in Ministry

For years, Holly served in our church doing whatever was needed. She never struggled for an opportunity to teach or strived to open a door of ministry for herself. She was fully committed to helping me be a better leader and to build the best church we could.

I have gone through some significant changes in my beliefs about women being in ministry. I believe that God has shown me that some of my earlier ideas were . . . off. Through that process, Holly saw opportunities for ministry in women's events, which have led her to touch the lives of thousands of women.

What if I had tried to prevent her from pursuing God's purpose for her life? What if I had maintained a view that kept her from being used to make a difference in the lives of others? I'm so glad I realized that it was time for me to release women from stereotypes that weakened our life and hindered my own progress toward fulfilling my purpose.

It is estimated that 61 percent of the congregation in the average American church are women. That leaves 39 percent who are men.[9] If I had maintained the ideas I had as a young man, I would have continued to limit more than half of the believers in our congregation from potential leadership—leadership in our church locally and possibly a greater impact in our world.

Holly has become an insightful leader. She has brought great strength to me personally and to many people in our church. Her discernment and her input have been invaluable in reaching our current level of ministry.

Jesus was radical in the way He included women in His life and ministry. He established new ground rules for women in His culture, and He set the stage for a new direction that affects us today.

Women in ancient Israel had their position in society defined by the Hebrew Scriptures and by the interpretation of those Scriptures. Their status and freedoms were severely limited by Jewish law and custom:

1. They were restricted to roles of little or no authority.
2. They were confined to the homes of their fathers or their husbands.
3. They were considered inferior to men and were under the direct authority of their fathers before marriage and their husband after.
4. They were not allowed to testify in court trials.
5. They could not appear in public venues.
6. They could not talk to male strangers.
7. They were required to be doubly veiled when they ventured outside of their homes.

The manner in which Jesus integrated women into His ministry gives undeniable evidence that their oppressive treatment, by the edicts of the old contract, was not endorsed by Him. He nullified many centuries of oppressive Jewish law and custom. Jesus spoke with women, which was not culturally acceptable in that day. Women traveled and studied with Jesus, and did ministry together with His disciples. He gave women responsibilities in His journeys. They handled money and helped raise support for His ministry (see Luke 8:1-3). Finally, He entrusted them with the responsibility of telling the greatest message in human history: "He has risen!"

He treated women and men as equals. He changed numerous Old Testament edicts that specified inequality. He consistently violated the rules concerning women. His treatment of women was nothing short of radical.

And after Jesus' death, resurrection and ascension, women continued to be a dynamic presence in the early church. Women, I would say to you that there is a place for you in ministry! There is a God-given purpose that you have in life.

I believe that the Church should set the pace when it comes to gender equality, just as it did so long ago. The church is the place where God's purpose is revealed. This revelation should impact our world. Church leaders should encourage women to be all they can be, all God has called them to be.

I have not always been so supportive. I was raised in a church where women's potential was minimized. I was taught the Scriptures in a way that held up a very different standard than the one Jesus demonstrated. I just didn't see it.

But I began to change how I saw women because of two specific Scriptures, passages that prompted me to re-evaluate my understanding of all other verses concerning women. I read about how the Holy Spirit had fallen upon the believers in the book of Acts, marking the beginning of a new era in the lives of God's people. The apostle Peter declared:

In the last days, God says, "I will pour out My spirit on all people. Your sons and daughters will prophesy, your young men will see visions, your old men will dream dreams. Even on my servants, both men and women, I will pour out my Spirit in those days, and they will prophesy" (Acts 2:17-18).

This passage is clear that God's intention is to use both men and women in proclaiming the Word of God. Peter said, "Your sons *and daughters* will prophesy." It seems to me almost as if the Holy Spirit was saying through Peter, "In case you didn't get it the first time—sons *and daughters*—I'll say it again: Even on my servants, *both men and women*."

How could I have missed that?

This gave me tremendous confidence in releasing Holly and endorsing her progress in the opportunities God has given us.

A second passage that clarified the situation for me is Galatians 3:26-28:

> You are all sons of God through faith in Christ Jesus, for all of you who were baptized into Christ have clothed yourselves with Christ. There is neither Jew nor Greek, slave nor free, male nor female, for you are all one in Christ Jesus (*NIV*).

God is establishing a unity and equality here in three specific areas: race, social status and gender.

There is neither Jew nor Greek = race.

There is neither slave nor free = social status.

There is neither male nor female = gender.

Greeks are not more important than Jews, nor Hispanics more important than whites. Whites are not more important than Asians, nor blacks more important than Indians. God does not honor black people more than brown people or white people. No. We are all one in Christ.

Rich people are not more important than poor people. Powerful people are not more important than marginalized people. Famous people are not more important than average people.

And in the same way, men are not more important than women.

I realized that my traditional interpretation about the potential of women in ministry violated God's intention, made clear in these passages. I could be the reason that my wife did not fulfill what God had called her to!

There are probably a lot of women who were not allowed to reach their purpose in life because of our limited understanding. We must respect and honor women in our world, in our families, in our friendships, in our church, in our community and in the business world.

I believe that as we bless the women in our world, as we encourage their full potential in God, not only will they flourish, but we all will. Women, you have a responsibility to love those around you as you pursue God's purpose for your life. As you move forward, be gracious with others who do not share your view. It is not respectful or helpful to the greater cause to try to force open doors that have not been opened to you. While I cannot answer every question that will arise about this issue, I want to build hope in you that God has called many women to various leadership roles. But just as a man can make things harder on himself by the way he approaches a situation, so too a woman can hurt herself by trying to force her way toward what she feels God has called her to do. It can be unnecessarily divisive to try to convince someone who does not want to be convinced. Be careful not to alienate those around you who are also trying to fulfill God's purpose. Confident leaders *earn* respect and trust in those they desire to lead; respect and trust cannot be forced.

Men can change the lives of millions of people around the world by bringing out the gifts God has strategically placed in the women we know and love. *Men need to do what only men can do so that women will be empowered to do what only women can do.* This is the exciting hope.

Thoughts from Holly

Although my role within the church has changed and grown over the years, I have always been passionate about the house of God. Philip never put me in a stereotypical box. Almost from the beginning, he realized that just as a two-parent home is the healthiest way to raise natural children, so a two-parent church is a great way to raise spiritual children.

But I *never* demanded a role. That is important to understand. I have helped where help is needed. I have cleaned the church, greeted at the door, loved the babies in the nursery, and taught in children's church. I have taught in services occasionally when needed. Wherever. Whatever.

Another woman in ministry once told me that I should demand to teach more, because that was obviously my gift. *Demand?* I think not! Too many times, women who have been discriminated against fight discrimination by being pushy and demanding. That is not the way.

I thank God that I was wise enough to marry a man who understands that my purpose on earth from God is as important as his.

To hear more from Philip and me about ways to discover and pursue God's calling in your life, you can see some short videos at www.godchicks.com.

Just for the Men!

Every woman has a purpose. Her purpose is no less important than our own. We are responsible before God for how we help our wives and daughters pursue their purpose. What if our main job as husbands and fathers is to ensure the success of our spouse and daughters?

Realize your impact on the lives of the women in your world.

What if Clark Kent forgot he was Superman? Can you imagine how much damage he would do just sitting in his chair or putting down his coffee cup or staring too long with his heat vision? You're the same; you carry a strength that can potentially do damage if you don't recognize the delicate worth of the women in your life. Offer words of encouragement, appropriate physical touch, the kind of care that meets the needs of your girls, and support that challenges them to realize their potential.

Men prepare the way.

While God has called men to lead in our home, He has *not* called us to lead at the expense of our partner. The gifts and talents inside her must be called forth through your leadership. Just like Coach Phil with Michael Jordan, you are to coach her toward success. You are the coach and she is the star player. You can lead her into her destiny, which means greater fulfillment for us all.

Release women to impact our world.

Women are oppressed around the globe; where their oppression is worst, poverty, famine and disease tend to run rampant. Setting women free is not only the right thing to do, but it is also the key to eliminating poverty, famine and disease. Biblically, there is no way to call ourselves followers of Christ while refusing to release women into everything they are called to be—including leaders in ministry.

Notes

1. John and Stasi Eldredge, *Captivating: Unveiling the Mystery of a Woman's Soul* (Nashville, TN: Thomas Nelson, 2005), pp. 6-7.
2. Ibid.
3. Ibid., p. 6.
4. Gary Smalley, "When Clark Kent Forgot His Power," May 12, 2004. http://gosmalley.com/when-clark-kent-forgot-his-power (accessed January 2010).
5. John C. Maxwell, *Leadership Gold: Lessons I've Learned from a Lifetime of Leading* (Nashville, TN: Thomas Nelson, 2008).
6. Keith Farazzi and Tahl Raz, *Never Eat Alone: And Other Secrets to Success, One Relationship at a Time* (New York: Doubleday Business, 2005).
7. Nicholas D. Kristof and Sheryl WuDunn, "Saving the World's Women," *New York Times Magazine*, August 17, 2009. http://www.nytimes.com/2009/08/23/magazine/23Women-t.html?_r=1&scp=9&sq=women&st=cse (accessed December 2009).
8. Ibid.
9. "Calling the Church Back for Men," Church for Men, 2008. http://www.churchformen.com (accessed January 2010).

9

Shift Happens

(Holly)

There is no more lovely, friendly, and charming relationship,
communion, or company than a good marriage.
MARTIN LUTHER

Let marriage be held in honor (esteemed worthy, precious,
of great price, and especially dear) in all things.
HEBREWS 13:4

A few years ago, we visited Seaside, Florida. It has to be the most perfect-looking town I have ever seen. People in this master-planned community, both visitors and residents, rode bicycles along the perfectly groomed sidewalks to the perfectly clean Starbucks, to the perfectly decorated stores, to the perfectly designed school, to the perfectly adorable post office, to the perfectly refreshing ice cream parlor, to the perfectly beautiful chapel, to the perfectly stocked grocery store, to the perfectly appointed restaurants, to the perfectly sandy beach—and then back to their perfect-looking homes or hotels.

As someone who comes from the city of Los Angeles—which is far from perfect looking—this was a new experience for me. Riding around on my bicycle in this perfect town, I felt like I was on a movie set. And in fact I was. Seaside, Florida, was the community used in the filming of the movie *The Truman Show.* Which, if you haven't seen the film, is about a man who is unaware that he lives in a totally controlled environment. All the perfection around him—nice as it is—is a total fabrication.

Unlike Truman, we don't live in a bubble.

Our marriages must not only exist but also thrive in the real world, with all its distractions and complications. Most of us do not live out our marriage on some remote desert island where we get to focus entirely on each other 24 hours a day. Nope. We have to work out our marriages with all the elements of life that come with being alive in the twenty-first century.

How do we do that and not lose sight of each other?

Here's Looking at You, Kids

Before I got married I had six theories about bringing up children; now I have six children and no theories.

JOHN WILMOT, EARL OF ROCHESTER

Children are a heritage from the Lord, the fruit of the womb a reward.

PSALM 127:3

My children are a blessing. Most of the time. It has certainly been work raising them, and there have been moments along the way when I wondered how I would get through that particular parenting phase—or if they would survive it! The miracle of it all is looking at their faces and seeing some of me, some of Philip and mostly just them. They are wonderfully unique individuals with their own purpose in God.

For many of us, children are part of our life as we work out our marriage. We might want to ship them off to Siberia sometimes, but we don't. The problem comes when our children become the center of our marriage.

From birth to 18 years old is 6,570 days. Obviously, our children remain our children forever, but day-in-day-out input lasts about 6,570 days. In contrast, if Philip and I are blessed to have a 60-year marriage (just 35 more years to go!), we will have been married 21,900 days.

6,570 days.

21,900 days.

Do the math.

The time our children have with us is much shorter than the span of our marriage, which is why it is not in the best interest of that relationship to make our children the center. They are a vital part, but not the center.

I made this mistake with my son, Jordan. When he was born, I did not leave him, even for a few hours, for many months. He was the center of my world. His needs took priority over Philip's. His cry was louder and more demanding, so I accommodated him. My marriage ended up on the back burner. It wasn't a conscious decision; it just happened as I looked to meet the needs of Jordan instead of my husband. Eventually, I started feeling more and more disconnected from Philip.

I had some ground to make up.

Fixing the out-of-whack dynamic was a two-step process. First, I had to get Jordan on some kind of schedule so that he fit in with our family instead of running it. (There are some great parenting resources out there that can help with this.) And second, I needed to go on a date with my husband. We needed some hours together as a couple. Jordan would be fine.

Over the years, we have learned that regardless of the ages of our children, we need time as a couple. Time away from them. Time to remind each other that we got together for relationship, not just the work of a family. If we don't take that time, our "communication" sounds like this:

"Who's cooking dinner?"

"Who's picking up the kids?"

"Did you sign the permission slip?"

"He forgot his lunch; can you take it to the school?"

All necessary communication, but intimacy will require just a bit more!

Do your homework to find a good babysitter and go out to dinner. Go on a walk. Do something that helps you connect on a regular basis.

We have also made it a practice to have not only a family vacation, but also a Philip-and-Holly vacation. When our children were younger, we might just be gone a few nights and then come back to get them before embarking on our longer family vacation. But eventually, Philip and I would spend a week together somewhere just the two of us, and then Paris and Jordan might join us. But that week alone with Philip would remind me why I married him! We needed that time away, just the two of us.

I have talked to some couples with young children who say they would love to go out, but their children cry when they leave and that makes it too hard. I understand that. I remember how hard it was initially to leave our children in the hands of a babysitter, no matter how qualified he or she was. But let me tell you what going out on a date teaches the children. It teaches them that the husband-wife relationship is a very high priority in the family. It teaches them that Mommy and Daddy love to spend time together. The best thing you can do for your children is to love each other.

We are to love our kids. We want the best for them. But making them the center of the family universe is not in their best interests. It also does not serve our world to have a generation of young people who think the world revolves around them. It will certainly not serve your marriage well, either.

We also had to be careful about how many activities Jordan and Paris got involved in. I loved watching them both in various sports over the years, but I tried to limit their involvement to one sport at a time. Otherwise, Philip and I would be so busy keeping up with their schedules that it would be tricky for us, in our already very full lives, to find time together.

As children become teenagers, life can get exciting. Just remember that you and your husband are one. Present a united front. Do not let your children or their desires drive a wedge between you. If you and your spouse disagree about the way something should be handled with them—driving, curfew, spending the night, whatever— don't disagree in front of them. Discuss the disagreement behind closed doors; in front of your children, present a united front.

Really, parenting is the procedure of teaching and training your children to leave your home and begin lives of their own. Might sound strange, but it is true. Our job is to equip them to live well.

Just as a confession: I am already working on my apology to the woman who marries my son. I failed. While he is one of the smartest, most compassionate and fun-loving young men I know (that's the part I did right!), he has no idea how to do laundry or clean anything. Maybe there is some sort of crash course I can send him to!

"For this reason a man shall leave his father and mother and be joined to his wife, and they shall become one flesh" (Gen. 2:24, *NIV*). Children are supposed to leave and parents are supposed to stay.

Thus, your marriage should be at the top of the priority list. Navigating children is fun, but it is also work. Don't let the work of it cause you to lose sight of each other.

The People We Bring

The wise man must remember that while he is a
descendant of the past, he is a parent of the future.
HERBERT SPENCER

Most of us have parents and in-laws as part of our lives. Some might be supportive and releasing, while others might be manipulative and try to control your marriage.

I have seen marriages seriously damaged because a couple did not know how to disconnect from controlling parents—and even from well-meaning parents who did not respect the new family. My goal is to be the releasing kind of parent and mother-in-law. I have some amazing girlfriends that have already walked this road; they are present in their adult children's lives to offer help if wanted, but they allow them to live their own lives. I have watched them bite their tongues rather than offer unsolicited advice. Lord help me to be the same!

We are to honor our parents. We are to respect and appreciate the position they hold in our lives. And yet, we are to leave them. Once again, look at this direction from our God: "For this reason a man shall *leave his father and mother* and *be joined to his wife*, and they shall become one flesh" (Gen. 2:24, *NIV*, emphasis added).

Your parents should not have more influence over you than your spouse. In the beginning of my marriage, it was so tempting to call my mom and complain to her about Philip whenever he wasn't acting how I thought he should. *So* glad I didn't go there. I'm not sure why I didn't, because I certainly made plenty of other mistakes. I guess I just knew that, while I was very grateful for the family that raised me, I had left them to begin my own family. And to do that meant that I couldn't run to my mommy and daddy whenever something did not go my way. Philip and I had to work it out.

Your parents did the best they could to build their home. Now it is your turn. Feel free to get advice from them. Take the best of what they did and use it in your own home. Just remember that you are building your own family, and their input should never create division in your marriage.

As our parents become older, there will be changes. Who will take care of them? A retirement home? Will they live with you? You are free to choose whatever you feel is right; just make sure there is dialogue about it between you and your husband.

Along with our family, we bring our past into our marriage. Good and bad. Each of us enters adulthood with a different background. And that background has an effect on our marriage; sometimes the past feels like a third person invading our present.

My friend Priscilla Shirer was a guest speaker at our GodChicks conference 2008. She told a great story that has stuck with me.

Priscilla and her husband, Jerry, went to minister to a local church. When they arrived, a little exhausted from the weeks leading up to this visit, they were grateful to get some rest in their hotel room. After settling in, they were awakened in a panic around 11 P.M. by the sound of a train barreling past their room, whistle blaring. After their near heart attack, they fell back asleep . . . only to be jarred from sleep when the same sound paraded by at 1 A.M. . . . and again at 5:30 in the morning. So much for resting!

When a woman from the church arrived the next morning to drive them to the meeting, Priscilla kindly mentioned that the loudest train on the entire planet kept them up throughout the entire night. The woman's face turned white as a sheet when she realized what had kept Priscilla and Jerry up all night. She apologized profusely and said that the people like herself who had lived in the town for years could no longer hear the train.

I'd like to suggest that many of us are the same way. We are so used to the voices of our past whistling around in our minds that we don't even notice them anymore. We have lived with depression, insecurity, jealousy, self-loathing, lust and pride for so long that we no longer recognize their daily impact on our lives.

But like Priscilla and Jerry in that little train-deaf town, a new person invited into our environment won't get much rest with all that disruption. What is normal background noise to us can be annoying or even disturbing to our partner. Hidden issues come out of hiding. In light of another's perspective, we are forced to face our issues. Our spouse doesn't share our exact struggles, so what we have successfully and temporarily mastered will sound like a roaring train to him. The past becomes a third person, invading our marriage in the present.

Maybe we had parents who loved us and loved each other, so we are confident in relationships. Perhaps there are a lot of us who have been hurt and betrayed, and aren't quite so secure in building relationships.

Maybe you come from years of abuse and are now on the healing journey (and it is a journey), and your husband will have to be patient while you walk it out. There will be times when your past will interfere with your present. It might be frustrating, but you both have to remain focused on what you are building together.

Maybe he comes from a single-mother home and really had no idea what a husband—much less father—should do. When you marry him, you are committing to encouraging him on that journey and working through the frustrations that come with it.

Maybe he expects a home-cooked meal every night because that's how his mom did it—and you have never even been in a kitchen. Maybe you expect him to fix whatever breaks around the house—and he has never even held a hammer. Our pasts, along with the expectations that come from them, *will* enter into the reality of our marriage. So be prepared to deal with them together.

Often our past will include a relationship or two. Philip was not the first person to ask me to marry him. He is the only one to whom I said, "I do."

Like most of us, I came into my marriage with a past. Not a sordid one, because the truth is that I only dated great guys. I never spent time with a man who did not treat me with respect and kindness. You know that saying that you have to kiss a lot of frogs before one becomes a prince? Not true . . . I wasted no time with frogs. Honestly, I only have great memories of the men I dated before I met Philip.

My memories of previous boyfriends are good ones—and that can be a problem, too. In the first few years of our marriage, whenever I was mad about something Philip had done (or not done), my head filled with thoughts of a past boyfriend who, in that moment, I could only remember as being perfect. I would think, *I should have stayed with* _____*; he wouldn't be treating me this way.* Not true. I had said no to that guy for a reason.

Our past, with its expectations and relationships, will have an influence on our marriage. It is crucial that we watch where our thoughts lead us. Stay focused on today. Stay engaged in this relationship that you are building.

What Friends Are For

*How rare and wonderful is that flash of a moment when
we realize we have discovered a friend.*
WILLIAM ROTSLER

Friendship is always a sweet responsibility, never an opportunity.
KHALIL GIBRAN

The friends we do life with have a crucial role to play in our marriage. They can either be a help and an encouragement or a drain and a detriment. The people you include in your world are so very important.

Most of us begin marriage with a list of his-friends and a list of her-friends.

This is good. Hopefully, you married someone who knows how to build friendships. And hopefully, most of those friends were supportive of your marriage. His-friends and her-friends, however, hadn't ever known you as a married person. A married person has another person to consider in every decision.

Before you were married, you might have been able to go to the movies with the girls without talking to anyone about it—but now you can't. Obviously you can still go to a movie; you just have to have a conversation with your husband. He might want to make plans with the boys too, so everybody's happy.

Some of our old friends might get frustrated that we have to "ask permission." (We're not asking permission, of course—it just appears that way to those who have only known us as unmarried.) Most friends will be able to turn this corner with you; eventually, most friends who started out as his-friends or her-friends either become our-friends or fade out of the picture.

If one of your girlfriends does not like the man you have married, her role in your life will and should get smaller. If she doesn't respect him, she will not be able to help you on your marriage journey and you need to let her go. This can be very difficult to do, especially when she might have been so much a part of your life; but now that you are married, your husband is your priority. Outside of your relationship with Jesus, this relationship is the most important one in your life. Any relationship that poses a threat to your marriage must be let go.

"Do not be mislead: 'Bad company corrupts good character'" (1 Cor. 15:33, *NIV*). I have heard it said, "Show me your friends and I will show you your future." If you have a female friend who is disrespectful to her spouse or jealous of your relationship or unwilling to grow in her marriage, you can expect that over time the poor qualities that possess her will begin to possess you, too. If you hang around bitter, disrespectful, unfaithful people, their habits eventually begin to corrupt your good character as well. We have to make conscious and sometimes difficult decisions to do life with people who are honoring God and honoring others.

Over the years, I have seen couples' friends have a huge affect on their marriages. There are two couples I have spoken to recently whose marriages were destroyed because of the negative influence of friends in their world. In both situations, one of the spouses spent hours every week with a group of people who were more interested in playing than in a life of responsibility and commitment—not the kind of friends we should spend hours with if we are trying to build our marriage.

Single people who hang out in bars should not be your or your spouse's closest friends. Men and women who haven't the slightest idea what they are on the planet for should not be your or your spouse's closest friends. Without a sense of purpose, we all make pretty stupid decisions. I'm not saying not to have people in your life who are at different places on the journey. I'm just saying that it's not the wisest decision to share your most intimate relationship with them every single day.

Are you surrounding your marriage with people and other couples who are committed to marriage in general and *your* marriage specifically? Will they help keep you on the path when you start to waver? Do you have a group of friends who, while they will listen to you, will not let you husband-bash indefinitely?

Women tend to be more relational than men, so if you realize that you don't have very many married couples in your life who can be a support to you in your marriage, why don't you begin the process? Invite a couple to dinner or coffee with you and your husband. Join a small group at church for couples.

I have a great circle of friends. Some are single and some are married. Some are newlyweds and some have been happily married for years longer than I have. These are the ones I open my heart to for input and advice. These are the ones on whose shoulders I cry when my season of life seems overwhelming, and the ones who can make me see the good in Philip when I can't.

I am in community with some pretty awesome people.

But I have to tell you that my friendships didn't happen randomly. I have built and continue to build them over the course of years. We have to *choose* to do life with people and continually press toward deeper levels of friendship and community. It's nice to have people in your life you don't have to perform for, don't have to pretend around; we all need people who give us the freedom to be ourselves, but who love us enough to encourage our best self to come forward.

Real friendships take time. They require an investment of time over the long haul. Over time, we discover the history of the people we do life with. We find out their stories, their struggles, their backgrounds and families, which leads to understanding the context from which they do life.

Real friendships take patience and forgiveness. The closer we get, the higher the potential for hurting each other—mostly unintentionally—which requires us to offer our friends the same grace and forgiveness we need from them when we mess up.

Real relationships with people who love you are worth every moment and every dollar.

I recently learned of a term called "collaborative divorce." It is a process that engages a team of experts to guide couples through the process of divorcing. A collaborative-divorce team might include attorneys, therapists and financial experts. Interesting. I understand and value the team concept, but I wonder how things might change if couples who opt for the cost and effort of a collaborative-divorce team put that same energy and care into restoring their marriage, perhaps with the help of a collaborative-marriage team (also called "friends").

I do not believe that an unhappy marriage is doomed to divorce. All marriages, at some point, are unhappy. All marriages go through difficult times, but things can and often do change. There is plenty of research to show that, except in cases where one of the spouses and the children are being physically abused, an unhappy marriage is better than a divorce for everyone involved.

In one study, it was reported that 86 percent of unhappily married people who stuck it out found that five years later their marriages were happier. In fact, nearly three-fifths of those who rated their marriage "unhappy" in the late 1980s and who stayed married rated their marriage as either "very happy" or "quite happy" when they were re-interviewed in the early 1990s.

According to the study, the very worst marriages showed the most dramatic turnarounds. If they achieved those results by doing nothing more than not leaving, imagine what could happen if they actually made an effort to learn how to resolve their conflicts, to understand each other and to improve their communication![1]

Your friends should be part of your collaborative-marriage team. Allow them to do their part to see your marriage succeed.

Working to Live, Not Living to Work

I have sacrificed everything in my life that I consider precious in order to advance the political career of my husband.
PAT NIXON

I can't imagine this was a good thing.

We live in the real world, and so our marriages must thrive as we navigate children, parents, our past, our friends and our careers.

Most of us have jobs. This is good! The challenge is to not let your job cost your marriage. If you work so many hours a week that you rarely get to spend time together, this will eventually lead to a lack of intimacy, which will cause you to feel separated from the one to whom you are supposed to be the most connected.

Of course, there are seasons when more work is required. If you are starting a new company, changing positions, planning a conference or working on a special project, you might work more hours than normal. Maybe while you finish school, he works days and you work nights for a few months. Fine. This just can't become the new normal.

God did the work of creation for six days and took one to rest. Making sure we rest and connect with each other is crucial to keeping the marriage strong. In our fast-paced world, this is not always easy—but it is essential. There has got to be time set aside to just *be*—time to stop going, going, going and doing, doing, doing.

On the flip side, there are some people who are so busy chasing dreams that they won't get a "regular job." In my city of Los Angeles, many are waiting for their big break, either in the entertainment industry or some other new business venture. Dreams are important, and yours may be God-given, but if your lack of work is hurting the family, change needs to happen.

Philip and I live together, work together and dream together. It might seem as though we have lots of together time. However, we have to be diligent about having couple-time. Our life together is so meshed with our call from God that if we are not conscious, our hours together will be all about work.

When we are thinking about something new at church, or when we are strategizing about how to cast vision for a particular project, or when I am planning a GodChicks conference, more work time is required.

We understand that about each other.

But there are times when we must stop our work thoughts and pursue the other part of our purpose: to be a strong couple. There are times when I am at home that I need to take off my pastor-teacher hat and put on my wife-mother hat.

You probably have to do that, too. I spoke with a young woman recently who was an executive in her company. She loved her work and was very passionate about it. All of that is good. The problem was that she did not know how to chill out at home. She found it very hard to relax and leave work at work. Not that we can't work from home sometimes, but she did it all the time. If she wasn't actually doing the work, she was talking about it. She couldn't—or, rather, she didn't—take off the super-executive hat and put on the wife hat. And this caused damage in her marriage.

Your husband doesn't want you to be his boss; he wants you to be his wife. Get good at switching hats.

Perhaps you are a stay-at-home mom and that is your job, or you are working from home so that you can be with your young children. Great! The same rules apply. You still need to take off your work hat and your mom hat to make time for you and your husband to connect, even if it is only for a few minutes amid the chaos of a home with children.

Maybe it's hard to go from watching *Blue's Clues* in your sweats and administering nap times, meal times and play times to caring for your husband in non-mommy jeans and expressing yourself to him in a way that captures his heart. I know it's hard. But because you love him and he loves you, you have to do it. And while he loves the mom you've become, he still wants the playfulness and excitement of the woman he married.

Get really good at switching hats.

Planted in the House of God

The righteous will flourish like a palm tree, they will grow like a cedar of Lebanon;
planted in the house of the Lord, they will flourish in the courts of our God.
They will still bear fruit in old age, they will stay fresh and green.
PSALM 92:12-14, *NIV*

The Bible is clear: If we want our lives to flourish (and I imagine most of us do), we must be planted in the house of God. Planted. Not just attending—planted, with roots going down, taking in nutrients, and leaves sprouting, giving off oxygen.

Planted. Learning, growing and serving.

Planted. Not moving from church to church.

Planted. So that people know you.

Planted. So that people can hold you accountable to living the God-life.

Planted. So that when life is hard, people know how to pray for you.

Planted. So that when life is good, people celebrate with you.

The Bible does not say we will flourish if we have a great job, a great house or live in a great neighborhood. No. It says our life will flourish if we are planted in the house of God. All of the good stuff, including a strong marriage, comes out of being planted in God's house.

My life revolves around being planted in the house of God. I don't just clock in and out as if attending church is an obligation or is doing God a big favor. No. I am committed to these people in my world. We are not just "church friends." We call it "doing life together." We are every-day, every-season kind of friends.

The theme song of the old sitcom *Cheers* says that we all want to go where we are known and where the people are glad we came. That's what happens when you are planted in God's house. You are known.

Maybe you are experiencing such pain in your relationship right now that loneliness is overwhelming you. You and I were created for relationship, so when there is a disconnect, we feel lonely and isolated. I have good news: "God sets the lonely in families" (Ps. 68:6, *NIV*). He brings the lonely, which is often you and me, into the house of God, to connect and to do life with His family! Connecting to a life-giving church is one of the best things you can do for your marriage.

Because I am planted in God's house, I am surrounded with people who are committed to making a difference on the planet. We are determined to build healthy marriages, because we realize that as our families get stronger, we become more equipped to make a difference in our world.

And that's why we are here! To bring light into dark places. Our churches and our marriages should be beacons of light that show those who are frustrated, hurt, lost and confused where to come for help and refreshing. Sometimes one of the best things you can do for your marriage is to get connected into a small group in your church that is reaching out into your community and the world. Taking your eyes off your own pain for a moment to focus on helping people will bring new energy to your marriage.

It's important to remember that life will never be perfect. And in our distracting, imperfect world, it's easy to lose sight of the main thing in marriage: your spouse! Make a firm decision that throughout every season of your life, you will keep your relationship with your spouse as the most important one. Often you will have to shift the focus intentionally away from your children, your family, your past, your friends or your job, back toward your marriage.

We can build strong, amazing marriages that impact our world—if we learn to do our one and only life well. And doing life well means learning to navigate the different pieces and parts of it. Doing marriage well means learning that, no matter what requires our attention in this moment, we will shift our attention back to what makes our marriage strong. Shifts must happen.

For some more information in navigating some of life's distractions, check out a short video from Philip and me at www.godchicks.com.

Just for the Men!

A few years ago, I was trying to help a young couple navigate their marriage through a rough season. He was in school and working full time. She was also working and they had a young child. Easy to see why they were having some challenges.

His solution to this busy season was to tell her and me that, for the next year, the marriage needed to be put on the back burner. I assured him that I understood what a busy season it was for them and that his wife certainly shouldn't expect date nights twice a week; however, if he was planning to put the marriage on the back burner for a year, he probably wouldn't have a marriage in a year. I suggested some other ways to handle their very busy life and ways to better their communication.

He wasn't really open to my suggestions. That's fine. Everyone is entitled to figure it out on his or her own or to find even better solutions. I don't know everything! But sadly, his solution—to ignore his wife for a year while he finished school—did not work. They were divorced by the end of the year.

There are plenty of circumstances that arise in life that can cause us to shift our focus from our marriage. Many of us have to raise children, handle aging parents, go to work and build friendships, all while working on our marriage. It *is* possible. We just have to get good at remembering what is important in the long run.

Children will eventually leave, so they can't be more important than the marriage.

Parents are important and should be honored, but your relationship with your wife takes priority.

Work is important. Please work and provide for your family. But don't work so much that it comes between the two of you.

Friends are crucial to helping us navigate our marriage. Choose ones that are committed to marriage in general and to your marriage specifically.

And lastly, please be a part of a life-giving local church. Being planted, not just attending, will produce a life that flourishes!

Note

1. Linda Waite and Maggie Gallagher, *The Case for Marriage* (New York: Doubleday, 2000), p. 148.

10

Give Me Five!

(Philip)

Men want the same thing from their underwear that they want from women: a little bit of support, and a little bit of freedom.
JERRY SEINFELD

A man should fulfill his duty as a husband and a woman should fulfill her duty as a wife and each should satisfy the other's needs.
1 CORINTHIANS 7:3, TLB

What the heck do men want, anyway? What are they thinking?
Are they thinking?
Is it something mysterious? Is it too personal, or is it something they've been waiting to tell you?
Women are often tempted in a silent moment to ask a man, "What are you thinking?"
"Nothing."
Now her interest is peaked. "Come on, what were you thinking?"
"Nothing."
"Are you thinking about something that is personal and intimate, something you're hesitant to say to me?"
No. He probably isn't.
Men and women are different, as we have said a number of times already. The differences cause us to misunderstand what the other wants, expects or is interested in. In this chapter, I'll attempt to help women understand (a little) life through the eyes of the men they love.
There are two major reasons many women struggle with relationships with men. One reason is the hurt and pain they have

encountered in past relationships, which they can't seem to overcome. We've spent time in a previous chapter addressing how to overcome wounds of the past, which I hope will help you navigate this struggle.

The second reason women struggle in relationships with men is that they don't know how to relate to or communicate with a man. I hope that this chapter will help you in this regard.

I am aware that you have needs that you hope will be met in your marriage. But this chapter is about the needs of a man. If I were writing a book to men, I would talk to them about your needs (in fact, in the "Just for the Men!" section at the end, I will be sure to mention a few of them).

The High-Five

I came up with a strategy for enhancing relationships accidentally, during a counseling session with a married couple. This session got so complicated and so emotional that I got confused. I was lost. I had no idea what the real problem was or where to go next.

When they looked at me with expectation, waiting for my input about how to move forward, I could have said, "What do you say we order in some pizza, because this is probably going to take awhile?" I came very close. Counseling is not a real gift of mine. Instead, I got an idea that has helped me with other couples—and has even helped Holly and me in our marriage. You might call this the help-me-help-you method (yet another *Jerry Maguire* reference), but I prefer to call it the High-Five of Our Marriage.

I asked the husband—we'll call him Dave, even though his real name is Rick—"Dave, I want you to tell me five things you need from your wife, Janice (her real name is Janice), that will cause you to enjoy your relationship more. What do you need for your marriage to be closer to what you hoped it would be?"

And then I asked Janice to do the same.

I also told them *not* to tell me five things they wanted each other to start or stop doing—just five things they needed. For instance, they couldn't say:

"I need you to stop being an idiot."

"I need you to close your mouth when you chew; it embarrasses me in front our friends."

"I need you to stop nagging me."
I wanted to hear admissions like:
"I need to know that you love me."
"I need to know that I am important to you."
"I need to know that you care about my feelings."
"I need to feel like I can go out with my friends to have fun and not feel like you are jealous of my time."
Dave and Janice needed a bit of coaching to come up with their five needs.

As one of them expressed a need, I followed up with this question: "What can your spouse do to help you feel what you've described?" And then I asked the listening spouse, "Are you willing to do some or all of those things?"

The sequence went something like this:

"I need to feel like you care about the things I enjoy," Dave says.

"What do you think Janice can do to help meet that need?" I ask.

"When I talk about my work, you could seem like you are interested," he continues.

I look to Janice and ask, "Do you think you can try to do that during the next week?"

And because Janice is not a jerk, she responds, "Yes, I can try."

Finally, I asked Dave if he was willing to acknowledge Janice's effort when he saw her trying to meet his need.

These five things become their priorities for the next few weeks—their High-Five. And off they went with some very clear and helpful direction, which they had come up with on their own. When we met again, I focused on holding them accountable for their actions and priorities while helping to fine-tune their efforts.

What resulted was an immediate change in Dave and Janice's relationship. They also learned a method they could turn to when things got messy (and in marriage, having messy moments is a given!).

The High-Five for Men

You might feel like saying in frustration, "Just tell me what you want! Just tell me what to do." I can't answer this request for everyone, but from the various marriages I've observed over the years, I have a fairly good idea. Here are what I think are the five biggest needs of men.

They are not in any order of priority. (The tricky part is that the man in your life may have a different list. That's where you come in. *Ask.* Be a student of him. That said, I'm confident that these are going to be somewhere in or near the top 10.)

1. Respect

A man likes to be with a woman who makes him feel respected. To be someone's hero, in some area of life, is essential to a man's soul. Respect makes us feel like we are moving toward the hero status. You can't have a hero you don't respect.

A man will thrive when he is respected. He will try, he will work and he will overcome many obstacles if he is respected now and believes there is more respect ahead. As coaching great John Wooden has said, "Respect a man, and he will do all the more."

Look at this issue from the opposite perspective: If a man feels disrespected, he will retreat. If he feels disrespected, this gap has to be repaired—even if he is totally in the wrong, is completely irrational or insensitive or is blind and oblivious to your needs. Why? Because if a man feels disrespected long enough, he may retreat forever. He will become like the groundhog that comes up to see his shadow, and then makes a hasty retreat to the safety of his hole in the ground. "I'm not coming out here to be disrespected anymore." It is also hard for him to ask for respect; to him, the need should be obvious.

If your man retreats from you through his work or play, or prefers to be with his friends rather than with you, take a serious look at this idea: *Maybe he does not feel respected by you.* Respect is the oil that makes a man's engine run smoothly. It helps us keep an open mind and heart. If you want to bring back the fire or keep the fire lit in your relationship, be brave enough to ask him some questions:

"What do I do or say that causes you to feel respected?"

After you have asked, then you listen. Really listen. Don't argue with his logic. Don't say, "That makes no sense." Instead, try this: "Thank you for sharing with me. I know that was probably not easy for you, and I appreciate your honesty." Then ask:

"Is there anything I do that makes you feel disrespected?"

If he's honest and if you listen and then make changes in your actions, it will open your relationship up to a whole new level of trust and responsiveness.

On a related note: Men like to win. They like to compete and to succeed. Most men retreat from a no-win situation.

A man who is not emotionally mature may express his desire to win by always wanting to be right, by being stubborn or by rarely admitting he is wrong. An emotionally secure man also likes to win—and that's okay, because winning is good. But a mature man will apologize and admit that he failed if he can see that doing so will get him a win. If he knows that you will forgive him, he will admit a failure or shortcoming—because making the relationship stronger is a win. But if he has learned through past experience that you will make him pay emotionally for apologizing, he won't admit so easily that he messed up. That feels a lot like a no-win situation.

Some men are called prideful or arrogant, but they just don't want to be put in a situation where they will be attacked, criticized or humiliated. A man wants to be with a woman who makes him feel good about himself and about life. How do you talk to him? What do you point out? If he thinks, *Others may criticize me, others may attack my efforts, but not you—you "get" me; I can trust you,* then you have his heart.

2. Encouragement

Encouragement is important to a man. I addressed this earlier, but it is so important that it bears repeating.

Encourage him for who he is—a good leader, a good friend or a good support to you. Affirm his accomplishments. Support his efforts in the areas that are important to you, whether it's being a good father, a faithful provider or a better husband.

Someone somewhere came up with the notion that men should know how to barbeque, to fix things around the house and to assemble newly purchased furniture. When did that happen? When were they giving out those abilities? Apparently, I was absent that day. I relate to what comedian Paul Reiser says in his book *Couplehood*:

> When you actually move into a house, you learn quite quickly how little you know about anything. Day one, the guy comes to turn on the electricity. He asks me one question:

"Excuse me, where is your main power supply?"

Right there I'm stumped. First question as a homeowner, I had nothing.

"I don't know. It's probably outside. Did you look outside, because I think I saw it there earlier . . . Okay, I'm going to level with you, sir; I don't really know what a main power supply looks like. What is it? Is it a big thing? Maybe it's inside. It's definitely either inside or outside, I know that. Tell you what—why don't you find it, and that'll be your first little job . . . You find it, I'll have it. That'll be what I do. You find it and do certain things with wires that I don't understand, and then I'll give you more money than you deserve. Is that fair?"[1]

Over the years, I have learned who to call when something goes wrong. Holly tries to encourage me in this area, even though I don't give her much to work with: "Way to go, Philip. Way to call that repair guy. That was fast."

Her encouragement abilities really shine in other areas, however.

The first Sunday we launched our church, Oasis, is a blank to me. It was a beautiful day—right up to the point I got to the podium. Then things kind of went downhill. I think. Like I said, I blanked it out.

That first Sunday, we had about 60 people.

The second Sunday, we had around 35.

The third Sunday, we had just over 20. I calculated that I had about three weeks before I would be giving Holly a personal Bible study. (No one warned me to not focus too much on the first-day attendance; it's common for people to show up to wish you well with no intention of returning.)

As Holly was serving as one our hospitality team—our "greeters"—I could imagine a Sunday very soon when she would say to me, "Hi, Philip! Welcome to The Oasis. I'm glad you came today. You are the pastor, so that's kind of important. I hope you give a great message today, because you're going to need it . . . and from the looks of things, you're going to be the only one here to hear it, anyway."

Thankfully, that day never came, but she has never stopped encouraging me in my efforts as a pastor, a communicator and a leader. Planting Oasis was a long process; it took about 10 years to develop some strength and momentum behind our ministry. *Ten years!*

Holly encouraged me all the way. She encouraged my work and my investment in our ministry.

But she didn't stop there.

"You are a good dad, Philip."

"Really?"

Both my son and my daughter loved to play basketball, and they played on several teams over the years. Between my son and my daughter, I rarely missed a game. I missed a few meetings, rejected some invitations to speak and left the office early many days. There were things I did not do that could have advanced my ministry, but I rarely missed a game.

After a long day at the office—I didn't really have the energy to do this—I went out to play basketball with my little son, Jordan. He was about six years old at the time. He would put his head down and drive to the basket—crashing right into my groin. A few inches higher and I'd be writing this book in a higher octave. Was this really necessary? Yes, it's part of the role.

"You are a good dad, Philip."

"Really?"

Children bring with them challenges to your leadership, questions you thought you'd never be asked, rebellious tantrums, and much more. They have a way of making you feel as if they know a lot more about what's going on than you do. They stretch you to your limit.

"I don't think I know what to do next. It feels like nothing I try gets through."

"You are a good dad, Philip. Most dads don't care that much or try this hard. Keep being there for them."

"Really? Okay. If you say so."

Holly's encouragement helped me believe that I could be a good dad, and helped me become the dad I wanted to be.

3. Companionship

Does it surprise you to know that men want a woman who can be not only a lover but also a friend? Men want recreational companionship.

Guys love a woman who can carry on a conversation about business, hobbies or sports. In a way, she's like one of the guys—but she's also a lady. We love a woman who knows the meaning of "calling an audible," "hitting a grand slam" or "getting a triple double." Men love women who can do something that can make her just like one of the gang—bowl, shoot pool, fish or play a game of ping pong—saying, "I'm a girl; give me a break." You don't have to be able to do all of it . . . just enough of it.

I am not sure Holly would have ever become a baseball fan if she wasn't married to me. But because she loves me, she has learned quite a bit about the game. She recognizes players, knows what an RBI is and remembers who is about to break what record. And when she yells an intelligent comment at the umpire, it just warms my heart. Really. It lets me know that she is with me, fully engaged in an activity that is important to me.

What sport or hobby is your husband passionate about? Try learning something about it.

Men love to be with women who don't take themselves too seriously. Someone who sees the humor in life makes for great company. To be sure, we want a woman to have interests that have substance, to be honest and real. But a guy is overwhelmed and turned off by a woman who is too high maintenance, who makes every conversation too intense and weighty. While I've made it clear that women should be treated as royalty, a woman who needs to be the center of attention all the time comes across as insecure, needy and demanding.

In contrast, a woman who is confident and playful is extremely attractive. There is nothing more of a turn-off than for a man to feel as if the woman of his dreams is totally dependent on him for every emotional need and has no life of her own. A guy knows that a girl with a full life, a life that doesn't revolve around him, won't get needy and possessive. She's more likely to be fun and have something to say other than "What are you really thinking?"

Two tickets to a baseball game = $100
A night out with the guys = $50
Girls' night out = $75
An enjoyable and confident companion = Priceless

A man also wants a companion who can provide domestic support. You may or may not be a great cook or someone who keeps the house spotless, but a woman who can add her touch to a home is a treasure. A good companion contributes her "special something" to the home.

4. Sex

Holly and I cover much more on the topic of sex in the next chapter, but I think it's important here to touch on the need of a man to be attracted to his wife. She does not have to have a perfect figure or dress like a supermodel to be sexually attractive to him. She does need to have a healthy appetite for sex, an ability to express passion and no inhibitions about making her desires known. Spontaneity, variety and enthusiasm get high marks in the heart of her husband.

A single woman should not sexualize her affection for the man she is dating. But there is an appropriate time in the relationship to begin expressing passionate feelings and a fearlessness about sex. This will reassure the man that he is pursuing a relationship with the right woman.

A woman who only has physical beauty going for her can't participate in a deep relationship—and an emotionally healthy man is looking for more than shallow, skin-deep attractiveness. He's looking for an articulate woman who has poise, purpose and intellect . . .

And also someone he finds physically attractive.

"Attractive" is a fairly subjective concept; what's attractive to one man may be . . . not so much, to another. But being attractive to your husband will probably always be a factor in your relationship. That does not mean that you need to worry about aging and losing your beauty or that younger women everywhere are a threat to your marriage. It simply means that it's important to care about your husband's tastes. Find out what "does it for him" when it comes to your selection of clothes, your hairstyle and the amount of make-up you use.

Yes, you *are* more than your looks.

No, a man should not judge you on how you look alone.

It may be true that men fall in love through their eyes and women fall in love through their ears. As much as you desire to hear "I love you" and "You are special to me," he longs for you to present yourself in an attractive way.

5. Adventure

Most men love taking risks. They want to get involved in something that demands something from them that is a challenge.

The kind of challenge can vary a lot and depends on the guy. He may be interested in outdoor excursions, starting a business or learning about the latest technology gadget. Whatever the shape it takes, it's about conquering a mountain—a mountain that looks like writing a book, starting a new career, launching a ministry, taking a course at night school, or traveling to another country.

The problem is that sometimes a man might attempt to scale that mountain regardless of who it may hurt, what the consequences are or even if it's ethical. That is why it's important that he is guided by strong values—because he *will* want to take on a battle.

And he needs someone who will support his adventure.

Sometimes the woman he loves presents herself as the enemy of a man's adventure. Don't let that be you. Love him. Encourage him. Challenge his ethics and wisdom. Point him to solid mentors. And support him.

After reading the High-Five of most men, you might be tempted to think, *Men are superficial. They just want someone to have sex and play with, who is pretty and will tell them how special they are.*

Hmmm . . . how can I say this?

You are not far off.

But if, instead of rolling your eyes, you refuse to judge his needs and try to meet them, you may be shocked at his response. If you try to meet his needs, he will go all out for you. There is nothing he will not do for you, his treasure rediscovered.

Our New York Story: A Moment of Glory

Holly loves romance. Holly loves to be shown that she is valuable.

I don't always get it right. Sometimes I feel "romantically challenged." But I get it right sometimes.

I think the basic theory of effective romance is that a lifestyle of ongoing small romantic gestures is better than a one-time "big event" of romance. If you never show any romantic efforts until the anniversary comes around once a year, your big efforts won't have quite the same impact as the "big effort surrounded by a lot of smaller efforts."

Reliance on the grand gestures is a little less significant to a long-term relationship. These tend to fall into the category of the less-than-glamorous, such as flowers after the husband blew it or a big gift to compensate for a stupid move or the "I know I forgot our anniversary, but look at this dress I bought you."

But big romantic events can be powerful. And—may I also point out—I got it right this time.

Holly loves love stories. She loves the movie *Sleepless in Seattle*. We have watched that movie many times. The whole story revolves around the story in another movie, *An Affair to Remember*, which is another love story. It's endless.

The basic plotline of *Sleepless in Seattle* has to do with misunderstandings or uncertainties in the relationship between the two main characters. They go through the challenges of any good story, until finally it boils down to, "If you love me, meet me at the top of the Empire State Building."

I don't know how it happened, but I was just sitting there minding my own business when I just started thinking about how much I love my wife, how special she is to me, and how I should express that same level of passion and value to her. So I got this idea and decided that I was going to re-create this same level of "specialness" that we had seen in her favorite story. I spent about two months planning and organizing this big event, and here's how it played out.

I told Holly one day that I needed to go into the office extra early the next morning. I was leaving around 6 A.M., so I would not be there when she woke up. So around 8 A.M. when she came into the kitchen, she found three envelopes on the table.

The first envelope simply read "Holly." She opened up the envelope to find a letter that said, "If you love me, meet me at the top of the Empire State Building." Also in the envelope was an airplane ticket to New York City. I had left early in the morning because I was already on an earlier flight to New York.

I told her in the note that I had our children's care organized, including who was taking care of them, who was staying overnight, and so forth. I had planned a ride for her to get to the airport. I had a hotel booked. I wrote that we were going to have a couple of days to get away and to enjoy each other.

The second envelope said, "Don't just stand there—you've got two hours to pack and get out of here."

The third envelope said, "Do not open until you are on the plane." In this envelope (although I did not have much confidence that she would wait until she got on the plane to read it), I just wrote a note that told her how much I loved her and that I was looking forward to spending a few special days away with her. And I signed my name. I thought this was important, because I didn't want anyone else to get credit for my moment of glory.

Holly says that when she got on the plane, she was so excited that she was telling everyone around her what was happening. This does not surprise me.

I had arranged a limo to meet her at the airport in New York. The limo driver was standing there in the airport with her name on the card when she got off the plane, and he played the soundtrack to *Sleepless in Seattle* in the limo on the way to the hotel. He took her to the hotel to drop off her luggage and then drove her to the Empire State Building.

I planned all this out assuming that she did love me and that she did want to meet me on top of the Empire State Building—unlike the movie, in which the hero, in my opinion, left too much up to speculation.

We had a great few days. I was a hero. I knocked the ball out of the park. It was a huge victory. It was like winning the World Series.

I even planned things for us to do while we were in New York. I planned things I knew she would enjoy, like dinner at a nice restaurant, a Broadway play, tickets to the David Letterman show and a Yankee game. I planned *only* the things I knew she would enjoy.

Now, the way Holly is, the more she tells a story, the more creative, emotional and bigger it gets. Sometimes she'll tell a story and I'll think, *Was that actually me in that story? I don't remember it that way at all. Did you go a second time when I was not included? Because I don't think I was the same guy who went with you on that one. Your version seems different to me . . . I don't really remember King Kong hanging off the building.*

But in this situation, it worked out for me. Our trip to New York has been a gift that keeps on giving because she likes to tell the story again and again, and when she tells it, she relives it. Even though it's been almost 15 years since we took that trip, it's like I did the whole thing over again just last month. And when she retells the story and re-experiences it, she gives me the "look" that tells me she is *so* glad I'm the man in her life!

Separating the Men
from the Boys

A phenomenon of our day is the confusion many men feel about who they are supposed to be. Am I supposed to be strong and tough, or sympathetic and creative? Which one of those am I being right now? Am I really a man? Do I need to change something about how I handle things to be a genuinely grown-up man?

The apostle Paul wrote, "When I was a child, I talked like a child, I thought like a child, I reasoned like a child. When I became a man, I put childish ways behind me" (1 Cor. 13:11, *NIV*).

Putting away childish things. What is that exactly?

Paul mentions the way he spoke and the way he thought. I believe that, if others are going to see changes in our thoughts and words, there has to be change deep in our soul.

One of the most recognizable parables Jesus told is the story of the prodigal son. This story reveals some distinct qualities that I believe can help men sort out the confusion they feel about what it means to be a man.

At its heart, the story is about our Father in heaven. Jesus uses a story to reveal something about the heart of God—and about the kind of man every man should aim to be.

Men often drift toward one of two extremes. They lean toward being weak, self-occupied and passive or toward being tough, mean and difficult.

The Passive Guy

Let's look first at the youngest son, the prodigal, who typifies the first extreme. He's the one who wastes his life away and finally returns home.

He's self-absorbed. He's selfish. He thinks, *I want mine now. I want to do my own thing. I want to be free.* Before he comes to his senses, before he realizes that he needs to make some changes if he wants to be a real man, he is passive. It shows in the way he thinks and talks. He has no goals. He has no direction. He likes to party. He wants to hang out with the boys. His life is going nowhere, and he's looking for someone to enable him to keep it up.

In our world, this kind of male is very common—we see him all the time. He's the kind of guy you can't rely on. He doesn't step up to the plate when you need him. He doesn't speak up for what's right.

We see this situation with Adam and Eve in the Garden of Eden. When the serpent came to tempt Eve, to steal humanity's birthright and to take their blessing, we have no evidence that Adam ever did anything to prevent disaster. He didn't step between Eve and the serpent and say, "Wait a minute, this is wrong. Let me intervene; let me defend you. Let me defend the Garden, our future and our relationship with God." His wife ate the forbidden fruit, and then he ate.

Adam was passive; he abdicated his responsibility.

We see a lot of men like Adam, like the prodigal son, in our churches. They are little boys in men's bodies. They are young boys in their 20s and 30s—and even adolescents in their 40s. He may look like a 30-year-old man, but he's still not sure what he wants to do with his life. He can't keep a job, and if he has one, he works part-time.

I realize that there are seasons in life when there is a need for training and preparation. A man may go to school or might intern for a year or two. But for some guys, this becomes their lifestyle. They're going to live a decade or two that way.

It's not uncommon to see a group of guys—13 roommates—who all pay $27 to cover the rent. That way, no one has to work much. This approach gives you plenty of time to play Wii and X-Box and express your art and go surfing on the weekend. Some of these guys would rather stay up until 2:00 in the morning writing "love songs to God" than do something that will make a difference in their life and in the world. How about being a provider? How about being a strong advocate for someone who needs you? How about setting an example of dependability and trustworthiness to the next generation?

I'm convinced that *boredom* is the reason some guys get addicted to porn! They have nothing else going on in their lives. Pornography and fantasy relationships are easier than building real, lasting relationships.

It's difficult to get up at 8:00 in the morning for a men's prayer gathering when you've been up until 3:00 playing video games and updating your Facebook page. He signs up for a class, but he can't even attend three in a row because he can't keep his life organized. It's weak. It's what boys do with their life. "I just wanna hang out and be cool. Don't put pressure on me, man . . . you're stressing me out."

Sometimes I wonder if this guy's secret desire is to marry a woman with a really good career and a nice house, because then he can keep pursuing his dream while she brings home the money.

If someone challenges him to do more with his life, his feelings are hurt. He would probably get mad reading these comments—but then again, he is probably too passive to read a book about personal improvement.

Now, don't get me wrong. This guy is a nice guy. We love this guy. We all like having him around. But the reality is that he rarely steps up to the plate. He does not make tough decisions. He tends to excel at making *no* decisions, because he doesn't want anybody to not like him. At the end of the day, he abdicates responsibilities.

It's like following someone on the freeway, whose right-hand turn signal is blinking. It has been blinking for 17 miles. You think, *Okay, this guy has the potential to turn right at some point. But I have no idea if he's actually going to make a turn or not. Should I slow down, should I speed up, should I go around?*

The danger in this situation is that some of the women we care so much about have fallen for these guys. I think some women confuse the love between a mother and a son and the love between a wife and a husband.

Some of you have said, "Philip, come on . . . I love him. You just don't understand him."

Women. GodChicks. Daughters. Don't make excuses for this guy! Yes, I do understand him. He's passive. He needs to be challenged. He hasn't had a good example. He needs something in his life that will push him forward.

Ask yourself, *Do I want my sons to be like the man I love? Do I want my daughters to marry someone like him?* Because he is the example your children will follow.

When men who are still little boys get married, there is a problem brewing. It's very difficult for a boy to become a man overnight. He often hurts his wife because he doesn't know how to be there for her. It's disappointing when your man just does not know how to be strong.

Sometimes aggressive or gifted women are drawn to men like this because they can tell them what to do—and they will do what they are told. I must caution you that I've seen so many women like this in the counseling office who now despise their husbands for the same weaknesses that first attracted them.

Passive men need to come to their senses, as the prodigal son did. They need to recognize what has influenced them and what example they have been following. They need to meet other guys who are doing something with their lives.

At the end of the day, they need to take action. Take some initiative. Create some momentum! Attend a class about business or ministry. Develop a special skill. Meet other men who are moving in similar directions in business, faith or ministry. It's extremely important to engage in productive activities and events with other men who are an example of strength.

As his wife, encourage and provide opportunities for him to spend time with men of strength who are doing something with their lives. Often, it is your influence that will help him become the man he was created to be, instead of the little boy who needs to grow up.

The Aggressive Guy

Now let's look at the other extreme: the older brother. He typifies a desperate and insecure masculinity.

He is the critical guy. He's angry. He's hostile. He criticizes people. He's the tough guy. He thinks that anything sensitive or compassionate is "girl stuff." He's not comfortable with hugging, kissing or crying.

If he were religious, he'd be the guy who knows all the rules. He'd be the guy who excels at keeping track of what you did wrong. He's the rule-focused person who doesn't have the heart of the Father at all.

Real men can laugh, cry, fight for something, win and overcome disappointments. We can do ALL of that. You don't have to be one or the other. You can be both. You can be strong and compassionate.

This older brother likes to boss everybody else around. He wants to give people orders. He doesn't want be *under authority*; he wants to be *in power*. His leadership is reliant on a title or a position.

These men are boys who don't want to take direction from anyone. They don't like people with a badge. They criticize their leaders—the boss, the employer, the pastor and anybody else who has authority.

He thinks, *If I was in charge, things would be different around here.*

Well, you're not in charge. That's because you're a jerk. Nobody trusts you. You earn trust by coming under authority and demonstrating that you are trustworthy.

Sometimes this is a military man or policeman or security guard. While I have a great respect for people serving in these careers, some men are attracted to these positions because there is a veneer of strength. Yet they often can't take the strength they learn on the job and put it into real-life relationships.

Many years ago, a man we will call Darryl came to me. He asked if I would give him counsel as his pastor. He told me his story and his concerns. After I had thought about it, I gave him my input . . . which hurt his feelings.

He was a difficult person to talk to for about a year after that. He was pouting. A grown man.

I thought, *Come on, you asked for my opinion and I gave it to you. You're supposed to be tough and strong. Put your strength into humbling yourself and growing up.* But his version of strength produced separation of friendships and broken relationships. That isn't strength at all.

He was a pretender.

Are you involved with a pretender? I hope not.

These men want to be strong but don't know how, so they get angry and intimidate people they can control and criticize people they don't understand. They scare their wives and intimidate their children.

What kind of man threatens his family? What kind of man scares his wife and kids? (Can you imagine the prodigal son seeing his father running down the road toward him and thinking, *Oh no, here he comes, everybody duck. Put on a helmet! Here comes Dad.*)

In the story, you can see the older brother's lack of true spirituality. He says to his father, "Dad, how could you throw this party? This son of yours—[Isn't that interesting? He's talking about his own brother, but he calls him "this son of yours"]—messed up. He spent all your money on prostitutes."

Mean-spirited people judge and jump to conclusions. I don't read anywhere in the story that the prodigal spent money on prostitutes. This idea comes out only in the older brother's accusations. That's what aggressive men do when they don't feel strong: They attack others.

Jesus taught us about laying our lives down to serve others. *That* is real strength.

The father in the story is strong—if only the older brother would apply himself to becoming like his dad! It's sad that the older brother says, "I've been here all this time" as though he is entitled to something because of tenure. In reality, he looks nothing like his father and has therefore disqualified himself. The older brother thinks he deserves something special, but he hasn't lived like the father at all.

The father is strong; he rises to the need of every situation.

He is supportive and releasing: "You want to leave? I'll let you go." He has concern and love for his son, but in his wisdom, he releases his boy.

He is compassionate; when his son returns, the father embraces him. He welcomes him home.

Men need to be able to express to those they love, "I love you whether you succeed or fail." Men also need to hear these words. Many men have never heard this kind of love and endorsement expressed by their fathers.

Even Jesus needed to hear the endorsement of His father. God spoke out of the heavens and declared, "This is my dearly loved Son, who brings me great joy" (Matt. 3:17, *NLT*). Jesus then carried out His ministry, with that declaration planted firmly in His heart.

If you are single and are considering a particular man with whom to build a life-long relationship, I encourage you to consider these examples of men that I've presented to you. Does the man you are considering lean toward the passive or the aggressive? Is he more of a man or a boy?

If you are married, it will help you to recognize to whom you are trying to communicate. In thinking about the five needs of men, those needs will look a little different depending on whether your man leans toward being passive or aggressive. Since we are assuming that you are in a relationship in which both people want to continue to grow emotionally, then at least a conversation about these issues, without making him feel attacked or criticized, would be helpful to have.

If you want to find out more from Holly and me about the needs of men and women, you can see some short videos at www.godchicks.com.

Just for the Men!

I listed the top five needs of men as *respect, encouragement, companionship, sex* and *adventure*. Are these yours? Let your wife know.

Women have needs, too. Her top five might be something like *non-sexual touch, conversation, honesty/openness, financial security* and *family commitment.* Talk to her and see if these are her needs. And remember: She is not wrong for having needs different than yours.

If you commit yourself to meeting the needs of your wife, she will open up to you. She will trust you. She will put more effort into meeting your needs.

In the story of the prodigal son, we learn about three types of men.

The youngest son is passive and irresponsible. This is the guy who would rather hang out with his buddies than contribute to building a home. Is that you? If you see some of these qualities in you, then there are some decisions you can make that will bring strength to your relationship. Women love to be with a man who is confident; someone who has a direction in life. It is important for you and your relationship that you have a goal, a mission or a direction in life that once achieved will make a difference to others around you. This will help bring strength to your relationship.

The oldest son is aggressive, critical, angry and focused on the rules. This type of man intimidates and tries to control women. Do you use anger to intimidate your wife and family? If you're a young, single man and you're still intimidating girls to go further sexually than is appropriate or God honoring, you're abusive. You need to apologize. You need to repent for how you treat God's daughters! Humble yourself so you can become more like the Father and not like the controlling older brother.

Is there a little bit of one of these brothers in you? Are you willing to ask your wife?

If she says yes, don't get defensive. Instead, ask her forgiveness and then look to the father in the story. Follow his example. Whether you are passive or aggressive, the Father's love will make you whole.

Begin the journey of being like the biblical version of the father—like our heavenly Father. Ask God to help you to be a man who provides comfort, direction, strength and encouragement. He provides for his family. He is strong and supportive, compassionate and forgiving.

Note
1. Paul Reiser, *Couplehood* (New York: Bantam Books, 1994), p. 217.

11

S-E-X Is Not a
Four-Letter Word

(Philip and Holly)

*You and I, for the last twenty years, have been fed all day long
on good solid lies about sex.*
C. S. LEWIS, *MERE CHRISTIANITY*

*I learned in church that sex is the most awful, filthy thing on earth
and you should save it for someone you love.*
UNKNOWN

Always be enraptured with her love.
PROVERBS 5:19, *NKJV*

We have good news for you: God wants you to have an incredible sex
life. Sex is a gift from God to us.

We're not sure where you got your information on sexual intimacy. Maybe you got some of it from all those wonderfully romantic
movies and now you are realizing, *Wait, that's not how it went for me!*
Rather than the perfectly choreographed movement between two people who know exactly what they are doing, with musical accompani-
ment and soft-focus photography, your experience with sex has been
more along the lines of, "Ouch! Honey, your elbow is on my hair" and
"Move over, I'm falling off the bed!" and "Remember what you did
last time? Don't do that" or "You're crushing me. It's not that you
weigh so much, it's just an awkward position." (And have you noticed
that in the movies sex is never messy? In the movies, why does no one
ever need a towel? What's with that?)

Maybe we can conclude that the movies are not the best place to get sex education.

There is a lot of false and discouraging information about sex. When we were going through pre-marriage counseling, I (Philip) was 30 years old and Holly was about 22, and we read an article about sexual fulfillment in marriage. This article said that women reached their sexual peak between the ages of 30 and 35 years of age. In the same article, we read that men reach their sexual peak between the ages of 18 and 23. I thought, *Oh great! I've peaked and she hasn't even started yet.*

There are a lot of ideas out there about sex that confuse people.

So many couples we talk to have had horrible experiences with sex. Maybe she was abused sexually and comes into the marriage carrying those scars, or perhaps he was promiscuous and now questions how he can rid his mind of the memories of others. We regularly pray with couples in which one of them has a sexually transmitted disease that they are now bringing into the marriage.

Perhaps you were one of the very few people on the planet raised by incredibly functional parents, who not only loved you but also loved each other emotionally and physically. They readily explained everything you needed to know about sex and answered all your questions openly, lovingly and without shame. On top of that, you and your spouse were virgins when you got married and thus entered marriage with no past baggage or relational hang-ups. On your honeymoon, sex was perfect because you were so well prepared and knew exactly how to please each other.

If the above is true, you can skip this chapter.

However, if you laughed with astonishment that I could even imagine there are parents like that because you are pretty sure those parents are mythical . . . or you got your sex education from your friends, who were *so* well informed . . . or you, like many people, indeed had a sexual past that you brought with you into marriage, then this chapter is for you.

Here is a story from Philip:

When I was a boy, my dad had his first father-son talk with me by calling me into his office. Already I knew I was in trouble.

Let me explain just a little. My dad was a conservative Baptist evangelist who specialized in preaching the exact temperature of hell and emphasizing the anger of God. We had never discussed sex on any level in our house.

On this day, which *should* have been the beginning of many great conversations to prepare me for one of the best parts of marriage, my dad called me into his office.

He had written the F-word on a piece of paper. He showed it to me and asked, "Do you know what this means?" Now I *knew* I was in trouble. I assured him that I did not know what the word meant. Furthermore, I had never done it and never said it to anyone. I thought that should just about cover my defense.

He went on to explain the activity, but his description actually sounded gross to me. I told him that I would never do that. (I later changed my mind.)

As you might guess, Dad left out a few details. I guess I was supposed to fill in the blanks by talking to my friends, whose parents had also given them a minimum amount of information.

After a few months of our marriage, with this comprehensive sex education under my belt, it should come as no surprise that one night (after what I thought was a passionate expression of sexual intimacy) I said to Holly, "That was pretty good, wasn't it?" and she gave me a half smile.

Not the response I was looking for.

She gave me the half smile that means "I'm not trying very hard to hide my true feelings." And there was a little too much silence. I could tell I was in trouble. I had no idea what for, but I somehow knew that we were about to have a very uncomfortable conversation. (I'm sharing this with you, but please keep it to yourself. It's embarrassing.)

When Holly broke the news that it hadn't been the most exciting eight and a half minutes she'd ever had, I was shocked. "What? That wasn't enjoyable?" I figured that if I was having a good time, everyone in the room would be happy. Nope. Basically, the newness had worn off. It was time to deliver. *Deliver what?*

How was I to know? I never asked. I had never had the father-son conversations that should have been ongoing and would have given me an idea of how to relate sexually to my wife.

It was a painful discussion, but that conversation with my new wife launched what has become a wonderful journey, an ongoing conversation that has lasted over 25 years and has produced a better sex life than I'd ever imagined. But at first it was . . . difficult.

I overreacted, got defensive, became insecure and didn't enjoy having sex very much on many occasions—and even wondered what the fuss was all about. I thought, *Sex is not that great.*

Before we dig into the topic of sex, we want to let you know that we are very aware of people (people like you, perhaps?) who have suffered sexual abuse. It makes us angry on your behalf that something designed to be wonderful between a husband and a wife may cause you pain or stand in the way of a fulfilling and healthy sex life. We are so sorry, and our word of encouragement to you is that there is a way to wholeness. It is important for you to get help. There are many places you can find that help—wise counselors, good books, and churches with programs that can lead to your freedom. Don't stay bound another day. Life is too precious for that! Sex is a God-given gift and is meant to be enjoyed!

The Sexual Prerequisite

Let us say now, so that there is no misunderstanding, that we believe the Bible's instruction on sex. Sexual intimacy and expression are for a man and a woman who are married.

We also realize that in our world today, many people just assume that single people who are dating are sexually intimate. Most think abstinence is an odd and unnatural standard. A majority of people think virginity is a condition to be remedied as soon as possible. Instead of virginity being a badge of honor, it is a reason for ridicule.

But we believe that sex is God's creation and we should follow His directions. Being married obviously doesn't guarantee great, passionate, enjoyable and heart-pounding sex. There are other essential elements. But if you want to have God's blessing, you have to start there. Sex is designed for marriage. This view has not hindered us or hurt us in any way. We enjoy the passion of sex.

Singles should look forward to enjoying this level of intimacy and save this very important part of your body and soul for your future spouse. The gift of your virginity to your spouse will be a rare but treasured gift.

There is power in purity. "Purity" means *uncontaminated* and *undiluted*. This usually signifies power. There is power and great value in *pure* dedication, *pure* strength and *pure* gold.

We can't go back and change the past, but we can go the rest of the distance with purity as our standard. Purity declares value, demonstrates a self-control that can be trusted, and protects your relationships from physical and emotional disease.

In Greek mythology, the Sirens' song is an interesting parallel to sexual desire. The Sirens are creatures with the head of a female and the body of a bird. They live on a rocky, dangerous island and, with the irresistible sound of their song, lure those who sail near them to destruction on the rocks.

The Argonauts escaped the Sirens because when he heard their song, Orpheus realized the peril they were in. He took out his lyre and sang a song so clear and ringing that it drowned the sound of those lovely, fatal voices.

When Odysseus's ship passed the Sirens, he ordered the sailors to stuff their ears with wax so that they would not be able to hear the alluring power of the song. Odysseus, however, wanted to hear their beautiful voices, so he had the crew tie him to the mast. The Sirens sang as Odysseus's ship passed by their island. Their words were even more enticing than their melodies. They promised knowledge, wisdom and a quickening of the spirit to every man who came to them. The song was more beautiful than Odysseus had imagined! His heart raged with longing for the Sirens, but the ropes held him to the mast and the ship sailed to safer waters.

The allure of sexual experiences is enticing and difficult to resist. When we are sexually aroused, reason often goes out the window; and unless we are bound by our convictions, we can be destroyed. Just as Orpheus sang a song so clear, we too must have a stronger song in our hearts to guide us along our sexual journey. We need to hear a song that will drown out the song sung by our society today.

The truth is that sex, which should be a gift to our life, will be a curse if it is not treated in the right way. While many people may not respect the biblical view of sex, our society's approach is not working. Chlamydia and Gonorrhea are two of the most commonly reported infectious diseases in the United States. The long-term consequences of these diseases can be life-threatening and certainly life-destroying.[1] More than one million people are living with HIV in the United States.[2] One-third of the pregnancies in the United States are unplanned and unwanted, and half of those will end in abortion.[3] Obviously, the way we are teaching and talking about STDs, AIDS and pregnancy is not effective, and the continual distribution of free condoms is not helping. There must be a better way.

There are dozens of magazines on grocery store shelves that offer articles like "How to Have Hot Sex with Your Boyfriend." Sadly, the vast majority of these are written by young women who haven't built lasting marriages.

We live in a society that tells us we are obligated to sexualize any feeling that comes along in our mind. Songs are filled with sexual passion. Movies present people who treat their sexuality as though it should be shared with whomever they are with at the moment. The idea is promoted that any limitations we put on our sexual expression are indications of a sexual hang-up. But the freer our world seems to get, the more sexually messed up we become. There are more sex addicts, sex offenders and sexually frustrated people than ever.

Great sex is not about how many people you have intercourse with, but rather the intimacy that occurs in a marriage when two committed people join hearts and bodies—the intimacy that occurs over the years. Although sex isn't the only part of a marriage, it is certainly an important one, for several reasons.

Reasons for Great Sex

To Provide Enjoyment!
We will spend a lot of time in this chapter talking about the enjoyment of sex.

> As a loving deer and a graceful doe,
> Let her breasts satisfy you at all times;
> And always be enraptured with her love (Prov. 5:18-19, *NKJV*).

Sex should be fun. We should both experience physical pleasure and touch each other emotionally at a deep level. The average person thinks that Christians are uptight and sexually repressed simply because we have convictions about guidelines we believe should guide us. But emotionally and sexually healthy Christians experience passionate, uninhibited, hot, laugh-out-loud, heart-stopping and jaw-dropping sex!

You can't take yourself so seriously. You have to laugh a little and play a little. This is an enjoyable part of life. You get to learn. You get to practice again and again. Sometimes you get it right and sometimes not so much . . . but you get to try it again tomorrow!

To Promote Unity

"Therefore shall a man *leave* his father and his mother, and shall *cleave* unto his wife: and they shall be one flesh" (Gen. 2:24, *KJV*, emphasis added). A man is to *leave* his parents and join with . . . adhere to . . . cling to . . . *cleave* to his wife. To truly create unity in a marriage, you must leave all other options behind, whether they are emotional, mental or physical. The only person's emotional needs you should be meeting, other than your children's, are your spouse's. Don't get exhausted trying to meet anyone else's. To create a unified marriage, you must leave the past and all others behind.

Sex is a unifying bond between husband and wife. It solidifies the union. When the rest of the world might seem crazy, when others hurt or betray you, it is wonderful to feel connected with your spouse. Often after a disaster, many couples make love because the experience reaffirms their life and union. They are saying, in essence, *We are okay; we are together; we are alive.* Perhaps you have a really rough day—a coworker takes credit for your work, someone cuts you off in traffic and points a finger at you (and I am not talking about the index finger!) and you run out of gas on the freeway. If you can come home and have sex with your spouse, the significance of those mishaps will fade—because you'll remember that someone is on your side.

We are not saying that sex solves all problems or that communication isn't crucial—but it does create a sense of unity. Sex was created to be a unifying bond and withholding it should never be used as a weapon or as punishment.

To Produce Children

God commanded Adam and Eve to be fruitful, multiply and replenish the earth. (That's probably the only command humans have had no trouble keeping!) So, yes—sex can and often does result in children. And we want that . . . but for too many couples, this is the main purpose of sex. The fact they have kids proves that they have been sexually active, but there is no unity, harmony or pleasure involved. Instead there is anger, hurt, frustration and misunderstanding. Those are not the qualities of great sex.

Qualities of Great Sex

Good Communication

First, we have to be willing to talk about our thoughts, fears and feelings. We have to be willing to talk about what we like and what we don't like. And we must be willing to listen without being insecure and rejecting the desires and concerns of our mate.

We know a couple who conduct marriage seminars. They talk about the number of women who complain to them about being frustrated sexually. Many women say they've never or rarely experienced an orgasm but are afraid to discuss it with their husbands. They are afraid because whenever they have attempted to discuss it in the past, they've been humiliated by accusations from their insecure husbands, who blame them for the problems.

Their husbands aren't safe to talk to. The wives walk away from the conversation feeling like "there is something wrong with me." Some women even fake their enjoyment just so they won't have to endure a difficult encounter with their husbands—but deep down, they are frustrated.

Sex is more than knowing where the parts go. Great sex takes open and honest dialogue about what you want and need. And it takes leaving egos and pride at the door—easier said than done. If you really want your sexual relationship to get better and better, there needs to be an atmosphere where both of you are free to share your feelings and needs without being embarrassed. Getting defensive will not help. When your spouse is sharing a need or a concern about your sexual relationship, listen. You are designed to meet each other's sexual needs . . . no one else can.

GodChicks and the Men They Love

There's a story we heard about a man who had a difficult time talking about sex. Actually, he had a difficult time talking about a lot of things. He decided to go to Toastmasters to build his confidence and communication skills.

In one exercise at the Toastmaster meetings, each person would get the opportunity to speak for five minutes on a topic that was chosen randomly for them by drawing a 3x5-inch card. One night when it was his turn, he drew a card that had one word written on it: sex. His job was to talk to the small audience of Toastmasters about sex . . . for five whole minutes. He gave his best attempt.

When he got home that night, his wife asked, "What was your topic tonight at Toastmasters?"

Fearing that if he told her, it would lead to more questions and more awkward discussion, he stuttered, "I spoke about . . . s-s-s-sailing. Yeah, my topic was sailing." He sighed with relief, knowing that he had avoided a difficult conversation.

The next day, the man and his wife went to the local mall. She went into a clothing store while he waited outside. In the store, his wife ran into one of the ladies they both knew who also attended Toastmasters.

The lady said, "I heard your husband speak at Toastmasters last night." She grinned slyly and continued, "Sounds like he *really* knew his subject."

His wife thought for a minute and replied, "He doesn't know that much about it. He's only had the experience twice. The first time, he got so sick that he threw up. The second time, things got so wild that his hat blew off and he never did find it."

Direct and honest communication about sex or any other topic will help you avoid misunderstandings. Communicate with each other about what turns you on, what turns you off and what your expectations are. Keeping the lines of communication open is crucial for making the sex part of your life great. Just communicate.

Honesty is another quality of great sex. Ask questions like, "What have I done that you like?" and "What have I done that you don't like?" and "What makes you uncomfortable?" Questions like these, and honest answers to them, go a long way toward building understanding and unity.

Many couples are frustrated about their sex life because they are dishonest with their spouse about feelings, desires and expectations. Our culture struggles with our opinions and responses to homosexuals who "come out of the closet," but married people need to be honest (come out of the closet!) with their spouse. Let your spouse know what you desire. Be honest about temptations, orgasms and what you like or don't like. Many are fearful that if they tell their spouse what they like, he or she will get mad or think they are weird.

For a man, sexual pleasure is fairly straightforward. Not so for women. And that is God's design. Because while sex is certainly fun and pleasurable, it is designed to create intimacy—and intimacy is not always straightforward. God did not make women like men; He certainly could have, but He didn't. He made the sexual needs and desires of women a little more complicated. Any male can go out and have one-night stands with multiple partners; it takes a man to do the work of creating intimacy.

It may be tempting for a woman to fake her reactions or responses. She may tell herself that doing so is to avoid damaging her husband's ego, but more often it is because she is not being honest about what she needs. Don't fake it. You are not helping him figure out how to make it great for you if you fake it. You have years to figure it out together, so make sure you are being honest. He wants to get a win in this area, so lovingly and patiently be open and honest about what feels good and what doesn't. It is unfair to him and to you to build up resentment toward your husband because of sexual frustrations you have never shared.

While a wife may be dishonest about her sexual fulfillment and her enjoyment of having an orgasm, husbands can be dishonest about the importance of physical attraction. "No, I don't mind that you've gained 50 pounds. It's just more of you to love." A man who says that really loves his wife a lot; he is trying to make her feel good about herself . . . but it is usually at the expense of his own sexual enjoyment.

A woman climbs into bed with her hair in rollers, flannel pajamas on and an I'm-going-to-sleep-in-a-couple-of-minutes look on her face and then wonders why he doesn't show more passion about their sex life. She's thinking, *You love me for who I am on the inside, right?* Well, of course he does—but it is much easier to express that love when she presents herself in a way that is attractive to him.

Generally, men are visual creatures. God made them that way. Not that women don't appreciate a good-looking guy . . . they just don't tend to be motivated sexually all the time by what they see, whereas men usually are.

A few thoughts from Holly:

When Philip and I are out walking, we often notice couples. Sometimes we spot a beautiful woman with an average-looking guy, and Philip will ask, "How did *he* get *her*?" Every time, my answer is the same: "Philip, while looks matter to us, what is more important is how we are treated. So that average-looking guy must be great at loving her, and that is how he got her!"

This is great news for millions of men!

Women are different in that way. Men are stimulated by what they see, which is why I do the best I can with what I have to make myself attractive. I want Philip to be attracted to me even when I am 82! I am the only woman my husband is going to have sex with, so I want to make it easy. It would be selfish of me to let myself go. I'm not going to get neurotic about it, but I will do the best I can with what I have.

If you have gained a significant amount of weight since your wedding day, I am gently suggesting that you work on a plan to get rid of it. *Of course* he loves you—and because you love him, you will work on becoming the healthiest you can. It is not about you looking like a supermodel; it is about you being the best you that you can be.

And, if you are still wearing those flannel footie pajamas you had in high school, you should probably get rid of them. Unless he thinks they are attractive. He probably doesn't, but ask. Ask because he is motivated by what he sees. Take him with you to the lingerie store and see what he thinks is sexy. You might be surprised. Why wouldn't you wear what he likes? Obviously you don't have to wear the scratchy lace bustier all the time, but put on something he thinks is sexy and see what happens!

With those thoughts in mind, let's remember that because we are committed to building this marriage, we have years to work it all out. Patience, in addition to honesty, is a good quality for great sex. If one particular sexual encounter with your spouse left lots to be desired, then talk about it and look forward to the next "practice session"! Sex probably isn't going to be a perfect-10 every time. Take the pressure off by relaxing and realizing that you have years to figure it out.

Willingness to Learn, Change and Grow

It takes work to have a great sex life . . . but maybe instead of seeing it as work, we should see it as an investment in our marriage! If you want to have a better sex life than you do now, you'll have to change. There is more to learn about sex . . . yes, even for you. Sometimes we act like we know what we're doing, but how do we know if we've never discussed these intimate issues with our spouse?

It sounds so simple—but if it were, people would have already improved their sex life. It's very sad that many people would rather stay frustrated, blame the other person or look elsewhere for satisfaction—which only leads to a whole new level of pain. Affairs begin and marriages are destroyed. This is the irony: Affairs take a lot of energy and creativity. If we invested that same energy and creativity into our marriage, it would make all the difference. Philip has said, "You can wander into an affair, but you can't wander into a great sexual relationship."

Selfishness is at the root of most marital challenges. Too often, we don't look at how *we* might need to improve, or we don't look for opportunities where *we* can change, and instead are frustrated at our spouse's behavior. Being willing to change and grow is essential to every part of a marriage, and especially sex. As we go through different seasons, our needs might change. What feels good might change. What we want might change. We need to be willing to change with each other.

I (Holly) read an article one time that described the top-10 things men want from their wives sexually. Rather than just implementing what I read, I asked Philip if he liked each of the things on the list. He was thrilled that I was reading an article like that, and even more thrilled that I asked him if the list was true for him. Turns out that only about half of it was true for him.

And interestingly, his list has changed in the years since then.

Just when you get them figured out, needs change! Don't let this be frustrating; see it as an adventure. Just as in our relationship with God, intimacy is the goal and it is more than technique; it is knowing the heart.

Tools for Great Sex

A Sense of Humor

The best way to break tension is to laugh. Not at each other or at the other person's attempts to please you, but at the humorous situations that can arise. Relax. Playfulness is part of a great sex life.

Creativity and Imagination

Eating the same thing for dinner every night would quickly get boring, no matter how good it tasted. In the same way, our sex life might get a bit humdrum if we do not apply our God-given creativity to it.

In today's culture, couples are encouraged to bring pornography via movies or the Internet into the bedroom. This is not the kind of creativity we mean. Bringing someone else into your bed, even if only in film, will eat away at the two of you working to become one.

But there are plenty of other ways to be creative. Turn on the music and dance in the bedroom. Put on a sexy dress to catch his eye. Really, the ideas are endless. We are not going to tell you *how* to be creative, just that you need to be. And whatever ideas you come up with should be something both of you like and are comfortable with.

In his book *Love Life for Every Married Couple*, Ed Wheat writes:

> I am suggesting that both husband and wife must use their imagination to fall in love, renew romantic love, or keep alive the *eros* love they now have. Remember that love must grow or die. Imagination is perhaps the strongest natural power we possess. It furthers the emotions in the same way that illustrations enlarge the impact of a book. It's as if we have movie screens in our minds, and we own the ability to throw pictures on the screen—whatever sort of pictures we choose. We can visualize thrilling, beautiful situations with our mates whenever we want to.
>
> Try it. Select a moment of romantic feeling with your partner from the past, present or hoped for future. As you begin to think about that feeling, your imagination goes to work with visual pictures. Your imagination feeds your thoughts, strengthening them immeasurably; then your thoughts intensify your feelings. This is how it works. Imag-

ination is a gift from the Creator to be used for good, to help accomplish His will in a hundred different ways. So build romantic love on your side of the marriage by thinking about your partner, concentrating on positive experiences and pleasures out of the past and then daydreaming, anticipating future pleasure with your mate. The frequency and intensity of these warm, erotic, tender thoughts about your partner, strengthened by the imagination factor, will govern your success in falling in love.

Of course this means that you may have to give up all outside attachments and daydreams about someone else if you have substituted another as the object of your affections. Many people who are not in love with their partner begin dreaming about someone else in an attempt to fill the emotional vacuum. Even if it is only in the fantasy stage, you need to forsake it and focus your thoughts on the one you married.[4]

You know that look women get when they want sex? Me neither.
DREW CAREY

The Right Atmosphere

Perhaps both men and women underestimate the importance of atmosphere, because atmosphere means something different to them both. Generally, men think intercourse, while women think kissing, touching, holding and hearing "I love you." The book of Song of Songs (sometimes called the Song of Solomon) should be required reading for all married couples. It starts with this line:

Kiss me—full on the mouth! Yes! For your love is better than wine (Song of Sol. 1:2, *THE MESSAGE*).

It's a good book! Each chapter is filled with ideas for creating an atmosphere of love and affection.

For most men, sex could happen anywhere and be terrific; but for most women, location is important. Atmosphere isn't just location, though location and timing are important. Privacy matters. Is the door locked? How bright is the light? Have you brushed your teeth? Where are the kids?

Atmosphere is also the emotional climate, and while the emotional atmosphere tends to be more important to women, men are affected by it as well. In Song of Solomon, both the man and the woman are great at creating an atmosphere conducive to love. Words are a big part of creating this atmosphere. The couple in Song of Solomon compliment each other and create a safe environment for each to express needs and desires.

We've heard it said that foreplay is really just forethought; 95 percent of great sex is above the neck. If a man jumps into bed, pumps the gas and never turns the key, his wife lays there with a dead engine—and probably thinking, *What is wrong with me?* or *This did nothing for me. Why is sex such a big deal?*

The key is foreplay, and that means thinking of her first. If a woman enters into sex knowing that her husband's goal is to help her have an orgasm, she will be very interested rather than being turned off. Men: Focus on giving to your wife, and you will get back just what you want: an interested, passionate partner. It is easier to focus on what you want and what you need, and while it is important to communicate your needs, great sex occurs when we shift our focus from ourselves to meeting the needs of our spouse.

> Give, and it will be given to you. A good measure, pressed down, shaken together and running over, will be poured into your lap. For with the measure you use, it will be measured to you (Luke 6:38, *NIV*).

What words are you using to create an intimate atmosphere? Are you complimenting your spouse? Using loving words? You can begin creating the right atmosphere long before you even make it to the bedroom. In Song of Solomon, the man compliments his woman and loves her with his words long before he touches her.

In chapter 4, he begins by talking about her eyes, and then he compares her hair to a flock of goats. (I am assuming this is a good thing!) Then he talks about her teeth being washed and that none are missing. (Good that none are missing, but you don't have to go into all that detail!☺) Next, he mentions her beautiful lips, her temples and her neck. He also comments that her nose is "like the tower of Lebanon." (I am sure this was an awesome compliment, but I don't know if women of today generally want their noses referred to as towers.) Later on in the book he looks at her waist and says that it "is a mound of wheat encircled by lilies." (Again, I am sure this is a lovely comparison for the woman he was talking to, but I imagine a woman of today would not be happy to have her waist and "mound of wheat" in the same sentence.) He says that her breasts are as "twin fawns of a gazelle," referring to their tender, delicate beauty. Are you getting the idea? All of these words were spoken before he ever touched her. And I am sure that after hearing all of these words, she was very ready to be loved.

Sometimes a man might say, "I am just not a good talker." That might have been a good excuse when you were 13, but as a man, you need to get great at creating an atmosphere of love with your words. You don't need to refer to flocks of goats or twin fawns, but you need to get good at giving compliments.

Gentle, non-sexual touches also go a long way with women. Are you touching her during the day? Kissing her? Or are you looking for sex every time you touch her?

In an atmosphere of love, criticism will shut down the moment every single time. This is not the time to grab his love handles and squeeze or to comment about the 10 pounds she could lose.

Not every sexual encounter between the two of you will involve hours of time, music and candlelight. Sometimes it will be quick. "Quickie" often means that he has an orgasm and she doesn't, because it's pretty rare for a woman to have an orgasm in 30 seconds. She's not designed to. Quickies are fine occasionally, but they shouldn't be the only way you have intercourse. There needs to be a variety. Mix it up a little.

Shameless Sex

One of the most important ingredients in a great sexual relationship is an open attitude.

> The man and his wife were both naked, and they felt no shame (Gen. 2:25, *NIV*).

Our desire is that you both enjoy the sexual side of your relationship without shame. We hope that the conversations started by this chapter will go a long way toward creating an even stronger bond in your marriage! Be honest and patient with each other. Relax. Have fun. Be creative. And enjoy the journey!

For a further discussion on enjoying sex with your spouse,
check out the video at www.godchicks.com.

Just for the Men!

The whole chapter is about sex. Read it!

Notes

1. "Trends in Reportable Sexually Transmitted Diseases in the United States, 2007," U.S. Department of Health and Human Services, January 30, 2008. http://www.cdc.gov/std/stats07/trends.htm.

2. "United States Statistics Summary" from Avert.org. http://www.avert.org/usa-statistics.htm (accessed December 2009).

3. Armen Hareyan, "One-Third of Pregnancies in America Are Unwanted," EMaxHealth, May 10, 2007. http://www.emaxhealth.com/89/11909.html (accessed December 2009).

4. Ed Wheat, M.D., *Love Life for Every Married Couple* (Grand Rapids, MI: Zondervan, 1980), p. 88.

Study Guide

Chapter 1: Mirror, Mirror on the Wall (Holly)
Whose job is it to make you happy? Why?

Read Psalm 139. Focus on the phrase "I am fearfully and wonderfully made." Why is it important to love ourselves?

We were created for interdependency, "mutual dependency," on each other. Why do you think God made us this way?

A healthy relationship is when two whole people come together as one. What happens when we look for someone to complete us, rather than being complete in God?

Neediness *demands*. Having needs *asks*. Do you demand or do you ask? How can you move toward expressing your needs in a way that brings true intimacy?

We have to take responsibility for ourselves—not ownership of the fault, but responsibility to grow, heal and change into an individual rooted in God's love. Is there anything you need to take responsibility for so that your past does not continue to dictate your future?

Go back and read the list of "I ams." Which one stands out most to you? Why? Be tenacious in making that "I am" a truth in your heart that powers how you live your life.

What does "virtuous" mean? God chose *now* as your time to impact the planet. What is He calling you to do with your life, in your family, at your job, as a wife?

Someone who can laugh at herself is comfortable in her own skin. When is the last time you had a good laugh at yourself? (I fell off a stage, remember?) Remember not to take everything *sooo* seriously.

Chapter 2: Victorious Secrets (Philip)
How in the world do you think Bethany Hamilton was able to start surfing again after losing her arm? Why do you think she would even want to?

"Sometimes the hardest thing about life is recovering from tragedies, storms and heartbreaks. The hardest thing is learning how to *stand up* and *position yourself.*" Is that true for you?

What were some of the dreams in your heart as you were growing up? How do you feel about the dreams that went unfulfilled or were even shattered?

Have you experienced abandonment? What questions are unanswered in your heart after that experience?

Abuse is far too frequent in our world. Is it possible to rise above such horror? Is it possible to love again? How? (John 4 can help with that answer.)

Jesus offers us relationship with Him *now*, which can be scary in light of our experiences. How can you engage your faith to pursue a present and life-giving relationship with God? Can you drop the past, not worry about the future and believe Him . . . now?

Do you believe that God's love is unconditional? Do you believe God loves you just the way you are? Why or why not? Have your experiences with other people's "love" made it more or less difficult to believe in God's love?

God calls us to impact our world through radical service, despite how badly we have been hurt. Do you think you can find healing through giving to someone else who is also hurting?

God is able to do more than you dare to ask. He is able to do more than you can imagine (see Eph. 3:20-21). Do you believe that? Memorize that verse this week, so that you will remember the power at work within you to birth the dream He has had for you all along.

There is a dance of victory that will release you into God's highest for your life. How can you find joy and "dance" even in your battle to overcome what you are facing?

Chapter 3: I Wish I May, I Wish I Might . . . Have a Great Marriage by Midnight (Holly)

What is it with us and the fairy tale? (Cinderella lied, remember?!) When did you realize the fairy tale wasn't reality?

Read Proverbs 24:3. How is a house (a life, a home, a family) built and established? What do you think it takes to build a great and life-long marriage?

Are you waiting for a miraculous event to occur in order for your marriage to change? What small tweak can you make that will express love (even if it's cleaning all the stuff off the counter!) to your spouse?

The statistics about marriage are not very encouraging; maybe we have a few things to learn. Are you a student in your marriage? Why or why not?

Think about the characteristics of your spouse. Are you the opposite of any of them? Is there a part of you that secretly hopes he will change and be more like you?

Questions help us remain a student; they are the natural verbiage within a relationship. When is the last time you asked your spouse some questions? Why not try a couple this week? What is he afraid of? Is he working in his chosen profession? Take time to ask.

Wisdom builds a home, a life, a family . . . and wisdom has a cost. What price have you had to pay for your wisdom?

Chapter 4: The Precarious Practice of Kissing Frogs (Philip)

Fairy tales are odd! How do you think a lifetime of hearing fairy tales has affected your perspective on love?

Aim higher! Don't allow just anyone to have access to your heart. Do you compromise when it comes to love? Why?

Remember the fish story? Do you ignore the red flags of risky relationship? Do you trust God enough to get out of relationships that could damage your heart and destroy your future? Why or why not?

Have you ever gotten too close too soon? Read Proverbs 4:23. Why do you think King Solomon instructs us to guard our heart above all else?

"Over time, you'll be able to distinguish the lure of pseudo-intimacy from the real thing." Have you started a relationship and realized later that the person was just not who you thought he was? Was he willing to grow and change or did the relationship have to end?

Similarities in a relationship are so important. What are some of your core beliefs and values that you want your partner to have as well?

Go back through the section on red flags. Which red flag do you find yourself often overlooking? How has your history and life experience taught you to accept less than you deserve?

We all have to learn to serve one another. Who do you serve—your appetites, yourself, others, God? What about your spouse or potential mate . . . who or what do you see him serving?

Chapter 5: Irreconcilable Differences (Holly)

What do you think about when you hear or see the term "irreconcilable differences"?

Does every relationship have irreconcilable differences? What makes you think so?

Our differences were designed to make us stronger, not divide us—but differences can divide us unless we seek unity. How is your husband different from you? How are you different from him? How, in light of what you have read, do these differences make you stronger together?

Jesus prayed in John 17 that we would all be one, even as He and the Father are one. What did He mean by this?

How can you, as a couple, work toward unity? What could you do if you began to focus on where you are similar, rather than where you are different?

Remember the story about the Human Genome Project? What realizations began to stir in your heart as you read it?

Make a list of the ways that you and your husband are different. Now, write a list of all the ways you are similar. Keep this list close to you at all times! When differences arise, focus on the "similar" list.

Chapter 6: You Had Me at Hello (Philip)
Why do you think dreams are so crucial to women? What are some of the dreams in your heart?

Every woman dreams of being truly known, loved and honored for who she is. What does honor have to do with love?

"Honor in the heart empowers the words coming out of the mouth." How can you honor and express admiration for those who are closest to you (remember the story about Michael Jordan)?

Communication is one of the most important tools in a relationship. Why is your tone just as important as your words?

Is silence an effective form of communication? What feelings and fears have you communicated in an open and honest way?

How can you communicate one of the following this week: *Interest, Expectation, Appreciation, Encouragement* or *Commitment*?

Why do you think patience is necessary on the journey of your partnership?

"Dependability is relationship glue." Are you the kind of person others can depend on? How about for the little things like respect, appreciation and support?

Has pride ever killed a relationship in your life? Where do you see pride operating in your relationships at home, at work or at church?

What do you think of Dr. Phil's quote, "Sometimes you make the right decision, sometimes you make the decision right"?

Chapter 7: Sleeping with the Enemy (Holly)

Conflicts in marriage *will* arise (we're not clones, remember?). Hateful words, indifference and neglect can hurt our spouse deeply. But how do they also hurt us?

How can being at peace with God help in resolving conflict? Do you feel at peace with Him? Why or why not?

Peace with God opens the door for deeper relationship with Him; that deeper relationship allows us to talk with Him about the conflict first. We can ask God to show us our part in the conflict. Do you find yourself saying, "I'm sorry, but . . ."? How can you determine to get great at saying "I'm sorry" . . . no buts?

What does timing have to do with resolving an issue? (Think about Esther.) How has poor timing affected your relationship? What about when you got the timing just right?

How about the place you choose to talk about an issue—why is it important? Where is a good place for you and your spouse to work through a problem?

"This is not about *his* problem or *my* problem. We are married. This is *our* problem." When conflicts arise, do you find yourself leaning towards *his*, *my* or *our*? How can you get better at staying on the same team?

How we handle conflict is also very important. Are you able to watch your mouth, or do you tend to say whatever you are thinking whenever you think it? How can you do better?

Humanism and materialism can both cause serious conflict in marriage. Have either brought unnecessary problems to your marriage? In what ways?

Determining to handle the seasons of life together will make all the difference in getting through them. Think about past seasons with your spouse (dating, marriage, having children, new jobs, moving, and so on). How did these affect your marriage? Are you intentional about spending time together and building intimacy in every season of life?

Communication is key—both listening and speaking. How do a person's words, tone and body language work together in communication?

Chapter 8: Purpose-Driven Wife (Philip)
It's not about you. Do you realize that your role as a wife is to encourage and support your husband in becoming all that God has called him to be? Do you realize he is to do the same for you? What is your response to these realizations?

Our spouse does not always encourage us in that way, and many women are asking the question, *Who am I supposed to be?* Is that the question in your heart? How have movies, media, magazines, family and church answered that question for you? Do those answers line up with who God says you are?

Remember the Coach Phil and Michael Jordan example? "I'm Coach Phil; she's MJ." How did you feel as you read that? Do you feel like you are getting the proper coaching you need to succeed?

Go back and review the statistics about women around the world. Were you aware of what is happening in other parts of the globe? Can you expand your capacity to pray for women everywhere as you continue to pray for yourself?

How can the church—and men in the church—take a stand locally to raise the value of women around the world?

Women are valuable to the plans and purposes of God. What does He say about women? What do the Scriptures tell us about women in ministry? You can start by reading Acts 2 and Galatians 3:26-28.

Have you experienced the freedom Christ promised to *all* humankind through your local church, or have you felt tolerated but not empowered as a woman?

"Men need to do what only men can do so that women are empowered to do what only women can do." What do you think about this idea? Have you had to shrink who you are to satisfy someone else's ego? Do you feel free to be a woman or do you feel overwhelmed or intimidated?

Chapter 9: Shift Happens (Holly)

Children are a wonderful addition to a family, but should they be the center of a marriage? Why or why not?

Do you find yourself talking more about the business of family (Who is cooking dinner? Who is picking up the kids?) than the relationship of marriage? How can you reconnect with your spouse this week to focus on building your relationship?

"Really, parenting is the procedure of teaching and training your children to leave your home and begin lives of their own." Are you clinging to your kids, fearful about them ever leaving, or are you preparing them to build a life for themselves when they leave your home?

Do your parents have more influence over you than your spouse? Does their input create division in your marriage? How can you take the best of what your parents taught you without letting their advice overtake you?

Remember Priscilla Shirer's train story? Did you live with anything (depression, bitterness, jealousy) before marriage that has come out in your marriage? Are you determined to not allow that "third person" from the past invade your present? How will you deal with your past?

How do friends play a role in your marriage? Think about your closest friendships. Do those relationships build up your marriage or tear it down? (If it's the latter, creating new friendships might be in order!)

How can you and your spouse invest in relationships with people who are also seeking God's purpose? Do any specific people come to mind? Who and how can you reach out to them? It will take time and patience, but it will be worth it! (Try joining a small group at your local church to build new relationships, if you cannot think of anyone.)

Your husband doesn't want you to be his boss; he wants you to be his wife. Are you getting good at switching hats (boss, mom, wife, etc.)? How can you do better?

Are you planted in a local church? Start serving, start loving, start enlarging your perspective, so that you and your spouse can grow together in God's purpose. He created you both to make and be the difference in a lost and broken world.

Chapter 10: Give Me Five! (Philip)
What do you think of the High-Five method? Is this something you would be willing to talk about and then try with your spouse?

The five greatest needs of men are: respect, encouragement, companionship, sex and adventure. Which feels the most difficult for you to meet?

"Respect is the oil that makes a man's engine run smoothly. It helps us keep an open mind and heart." Be brave enough this week to ask your husband the following two questions: (1) "What do I do or say that causes you to feel respected?" and (2) "Is there anything I do that makes you feel disrespected?"

Is encouragement operating freely in your relationship? What are some ways you encourage your husband? How can you begin to consistently encourage who he is, his efforts, his work and his ministry?

Do you take time to "play" with your husband? Are you his companion? If not, what are his hobbies? What does he love? How can you get involved?

What is attractive to your husband? You should not be valued only for how you look, but it is okay for your husband to care about your appearance. How can you get great at meeting his desire in this area?

Are you an enemy to your spouse's adventure or a support to his adventure? Does the pursuit of adventure scare you?

There is so much confusion today about who men are supposed to be. What has been your experience at home, at work and at church with passive or aggressive men? If you are single, do you tend to attract one over the other? Are there some unhealthy traits in you that make you attracted to an unhealthy male?

Did you ever consider the Prodigal Son story as it was described in this chapter? How does the love of the Father affect you?

Chapter 11: S-E-X Is Not a Four-Letter Word (Philip and Holly)

Note: These questions should be discussed by a husband and wife!

Where did you get your information about sex? Was it helpful or was it something you had to overcome?

"Sex, which should be a gift to our life, will be a curse if it is not treated in the right way. While many people may not respect the biblical view of sex, our society's approach is not working." What do you think of these ideas?

Are you comfortable talking with your spouse about sex, about what you like and don't like? Have you gotten defensive about it instead of listening?

Wives, are you faking your responses? If so, why? Why is it hard to be honest about what you need?

As we go through different seasons in life, our needs might change. Are you talking about those changes?

How can you use your imagination to spice up your sex life? Spend some time this week brainstorming ways to make your love life with your spouse sizzle.

What can you do to create a better atmosphere? What kind of foreplay are you expecting? What words are you using to create an intimate atmosphere?

How many non-sexual touches did you give each other today? Try more tomorrow!

GodChicks

For more information on the annual GodChicks Women's Conference, Events & Media, please visit GodChicks.com